TABLE OF CONTENTS

CHAPTER-1

INTRODUCTION TO BULLION MARKET - AN OVERVIEW

1.1 INTRODUCTION TO BULLION MARKET

Bullion is gold, silver, or other precious metals in the form of bars or ingots. Bullion is used for trade on a market. The word "bullion" comes from the old French word "bouillon" which meant "boiling", and was the term used to describe the activity of a melting house. The value of bullion is determined by the value of its precious metals content which is defined by its purity and frame. To assess the purity of gold bullion, the centuries old technique of fire assay is still employed, together with modern spectroscopic instrumentation, to accurately determine its quality to ensure the owner receives fair market value for it. It is also weighed extremely accurately.

Trading of gold is known as bullion trading. India is the leading consumer and importer of gold in the world. Due to this, the potential of the India bullion market is very promising. Owing to the weak price of Dollar in the global market, the price of bullion is soaring. The gem and jewelry industry of India is one of the fastest growing sectors of the economy at an approximate rate of 15%. The India Bullion market is under the strict supervision of the Government as bullion is one of the major indicators of the wealth of the country. Thus, the bullion reserve of a country is the indicator of the amount of wealth a country possesses. India Bullion Market is a recognizable index that highlights the economic growth of the nation. India is the leading consumer and importer of gold in the world as a result of which the potential of the Indian bullion market is very promising.

The two major economic functions of a gold futures market are price risk management and price discovery. There is enormous flow of foreign exchange investment avenues in the country due to increased integration of national financial markets with the international market. Trading in commodity futures contracts can be very risky for the inexperienced. One cause of this risk is the high amount of leverage generally involved in holding futures contracts. Gold derivatives market has differed from that of other commodities due to the existence of massive above-ground stocks. This has made the gold market both operate in a different fashion from those relating to other commodities and become considerably more extensive. It has brought to market participants both new opportunities and new risks. As with all derivative markets, its complexity, the rapid pace of innovation and the chain of transactions typically triggered by one initial operation have made it difficult to measure or assess the market.

Gold is used for different purposes and these certainly include commodity uses. Industrial applications of gold account for about 10 percent of demand each year. Demand for gold as jewellery absorbs around 75 percent of the gold supplied to the market each year, with the balance made up by investment. Gold is certainly included in the leading tradable commodity indices. That makes gold, for many practical purposes, as a commodity. The real value of gold is not that it provides a quick, speculative fix, but that it can provide a sure and steady means of protecting wealth and enhance the consistency of returns.

Gold is unusual because it's both a commodity and a monetary asset and is an effective diversifier because its performance tends to move independently of other investments. The real value of gold is not that it provides a quick, speculative fix, but that it can provide a sure and steady means of protecting wealth and enhance the consistency of returns. For centuries gold has been used as a store of value. When viewed from the historical perspective of a multi-century time frame, no other investment has the wealth preserving power of gold. Other assets are dependent upon a certain government or political climate to retain value or appreciate, but gold is largely independent of political climate.

Demand for investment gold (bars, coins and medals) has picked up in recent years, accounting for some 37 percent of end-use consumption in 2011 a clear sign that the retail end of the market has invested in gold as a means to safeguard wealth against the potential for the financial crisis to escalate. Even in Asia, where gold jewellery has a dual use of an adornment and as an item of wealth/investment, demand for gold bars has picked up.

However, in many cases the value of gold moves indirectly with the strength of the economy. When the economy is doing well and growing, gold prices tend to fall and vice versa when the economy contracts. That said, many macroeconomic variables exhibited in growing and contracting economies play a greater role in influencing the price of gold. These factors include interest rates, oil prices, inflation and the foreign exchange market. The Gold Reserve Act of 1934 gave the government the power to peg the value of the dollar to gold and adjust it as it pleased. Normally the nationalization of a commodity would have been a huge controversy, but the Gold Reserve Act was seen as a necessary step to ending the Great Depression. The U.S. dollar is another primary factor that drives prices in the gold industry. There is generally an inverse relation between the price of gold and the value of the U.S. dollar.

According to Merriam-Webster Dictionary, "Bullion is gold, silver, or other precious metals in the form of bars or ingots. Typically, bullion is used for trade on a market. The word "bullion" comes from the old French word bouillon, which meant "boiling", and was the term used to describe the activity of a melting house."[1]

According to Dictionary.Com, "Bullion is a commodity that investors may use as a hedge against recession and inflation. Thus, while it is volatile like most commodities, it always maintains a relatively high value."[2]

1.2 DESCRIBING THE CONCEPT BULLION MARKET

Bullion market is a market where traders trade in precious metals like gold and silver. This is a place where exchanges of gold and silver take place over the counter and in the futures market. Trading in bullions market is open 24 hours. Bullion markets exist across the globe and most of the transactions take place through electronic means or by phone. The versatile uses of silver and gold in many areas especially its industrial applications decide the prices of the precious metal. Bullions are considered as a safe bet to hedge against inflation or as a safe haven for investment.

---

[1] Merriam-Webster Dictionary: Bullion - Definition, Access date between May 10, 2014 to May 11, 2014, from http://www.merriam-webster.com/dictionary/bullion

[2] Dictionary.Com: Bullion – Definition, Access date between April 17, 2013 to April 19, 2013, from https://www.dictionary.com/browse/bullion

There are other avenues to invest in these markets such as Exchange Traded Funds (ETFs), which allow greater flexibility as far as safety and storage issues are concerned. There are a significant number of Gold ETFs available in the market, and the SPDR Gold Trust (GLD) is the most significant gold exchange-traded fund as of November 30, 2017. The primary disadvantage of trading in physical bullion is that it is difficult to store the metal, as there is always a risk of theft associated with it. A bullion market has a lot of active players like banks, fabricators, refiners, vault operators, jewelers, hedgers, arbitrageurs, and speculators, etc. The brokers also facilitate the transactions between parties of two different countries or places. Investing in gold has always been a traditional route for investing. The simple market mechanism for investing in gold is to invest when the price is low and sell the investment when the market is at high. Bullions tend to move at an erratic pace and have different behavioral patterns when compared to the other market securities like equities and funds. This makes it a better bet for hedging and makes it a worthy asset.

A bullion market is a market through which buyers and sellers trade gold and silver as well as associated derivatives.[3] The London bullion market is a wholesale over-the-counter market for the trading of gold and silver. Trading is conducted amongst members of the London Bullion Market Association (LBMA), loosely overseen by the Bank of England. Most of the members are major international banks or bullion dealers and refiners.[4]

The London bullion market is the most globally traded market. It deals in gold and silver in futures, options and forwards contracts. The London Bullion Market Association oversees the operations of this bullion market, and it has set specific standards about the quality of the metals transacted. The London bullion market has over 150 members from 30 countries. These members derive majority of the revenue from Gold and Silver bullion trading. The bullion market is also subject to market fluctuations like any another market related security. Investors view bullion trading as a safe haven to hedge against inflation.

---

[3] Investopedia: Bullion market, Access date between June 10, 2015 to June 14, 2015, from https://www.investopedia.com/terms/b/bullion-market.asp

[4] London Bullion Market, Access date between January 10, 2016 to January 15, 2016, from https://en.wikipedia.org/wiki/London_bullion_market

1.3 SIGNIFICANCE OF BULLION MARKET

Bullion market plays an important role in the pricing of gold and silver all around the world. A range of professional market participants is active in the bullion markets, such as banks, fabricators, refiners, and vault operators or transport companies, as well as brokers. They provide facilities for the refining, melting, assaying, transporting, trading, and vaulting of gold and silver bullion. Bullion trading is the basic term given to trading of gold, and the bullion reserve of a country demonstrates how much wealth a country has. Since India is the world's largest importer and consumer of gold on the planet, its bullion market has a lot of promise. As a matter of fact, bullion's price is on the rise thanks to a decline in the value of the dollar in the international market.

Besides the direct bullion market participants, other professional parties such as investment companies and jewelers use bullion in the context of products or services which they produce or offer to customers. For example, shares of the world's largest gold exchange-traded fund, the SPDR Gold Shares, represents ownership in vaulted gold bullion. Private individuals use bullion primarily as an investment or potential store of value. Gold bullion and silver bullion are the most important forms of physical precious metals investments. Bullion investments can be considered as insurance against inflation or economic turmoil and may not entail direct counterparty risk.

Compared to numismatic coins, bullion bars or bullion coins can typically be purchased and traded at lower margins and their trading prices are closer to the values of the contained precious metals. Gold is being appreciated in India as a secondary source of investment after bank deposits. India is the major investor in gold jewelers. Domestic consumption is sensitive to monsoon, harvest and marriage seasons. Indian jewelers off take is sensitive to price increases and more so to instability. Therefore the Bullion Market in India even after undergoing several corrections has retained its status of being a familiar index highlighting the financial growth of the nation in recent times.

Gold and silver are the most enduring form of currency and investment in the world. If you want to buy paper money today, you can expect it to be worth the same exact amount (at least on paper) in 20 years. If you buy gold or silver, however, you have a very reasonable chance of seeing your investment multiply when measured in dollars. This is the difference between investing money and having money.

The reason that countries have become so interested in owning precious metals relates directly to their confidence levels in worldwide currencies. If a government is given the choice of having assets in the form of a currency that has the potential to become worthless or gold and silver which has sustained significant value for thousands of years, you can see why they have been going to metals more and more frequently as the years go by.

One of the most active times for gold and silver trading is when there is economic worry. Though the exact correlation is debated among economic experts, many feel that metals are one of the safest bets in a time of uncertainty. With that said, however, the past 100 years have seen many sizable runs in many directions in both the gold and silver markets. While unusual economic conditions can certainly spur big movements in the world of precious metals, they are not an absolute requirement.

In the 1980s and 2000s, both periods that sustained noteworthy economic troubles, gold and silver both saw significant gains. Now, the difference between these two time periods is also important to note. Unlike in the 1980s, the collapse of gold and silver in the late 2000s was not dramatic, and it in fact regained much of its initial losses in the months. This is one of the primary differences between a pullback and a total bubble. Gold and silver have recovered most of their latest pullback and remain steady. If there is one thing that almost every chart shows, it is that gold and silver have always been one of the safest places to put your money in times of economic distress.

The export and import of gold has witnessed an increase in the number of restrictions in comparison with other commodities. India's bullion market is highly fragmented and bullion prices vary to significant extents in various parts of the country, and the lack of a common benchmark across the nation is cited as the primary reason for its unorganized bullion market.

1.4 BULLION MARKET IN THE INDIAN ECONOMY

India Bullion Market is a recognizable index that highlights the economic growth of the nation. India is now, according to The World Gold Council (WGC), the world's second biggest consumer of gold having been surpassed by China. However, India remains a major player in the gold market. For Indians gold is auspicious. It is a sacred metal, an embodiment of divinity that is used to adorn the body and celebrate the householder's life. Gold in India is considered the metal form of Lakshmi, the goddess of wealth. Gold coins are worshipped with flowers and incense during harvest festivals. Buying gold is a popular activity on Akshaya Tritiya, as it is the ultimate symbol of wealth and prosperity. Gold and gold jewelry bought and worn on this day signify never diminishing good fortune.

Gold demand in India witnessed a significant decline of 21% in 2016 at 675.5 tonne, mainly due to challenges like jewellers strike, PAN card requirement and demonetisation move, says World Gold Council. The gold demand for 2015 stood at 857.2 tonne, the WGC data revealed. Jewellery demand in the country also witnessed a sharp decline of 22.4% in 2016, at 514 tonne compared to 662.3 tonnes in 2015. In value terms, jewellery demand saw a drop of 12.3% in 2016 at Rs1,38,837.8 crore, from Rs1,58,310.4 crore in 2015, the report revealed.[5]

In India, gold is religion. India's love affair with gold is timeless, spanning century's even millennia. Roman historian, Pliny, lamented some 1800 years ago, how India, the sink of precious metals, was draining Rome of gold, an appellation that resonates even today. Indians see the metal as a symbol of purity, prosperity and good fortune. Although estimates vary, India is now thought to hold close to 18,000 tonnes or 10% of the world's entire above-ground gold stocks. Seven percent of India's total household savings is currently held in gold. Gold purchase in India is entwined with religious and cultural beliefs.

---

[5] HT Media Ltd.: India's gold demand in 2016: World Gold Council report, Access date between October 13, 2014 to October 16, 2014, from https://www.livemint.com/Money

According to the WGC, in the last decade, 75% of gold demand in India has taken the form of jewelry. Also, according to the WGC, "To make a distinction between investment and jewelry demand is to misunderstand Indian attitudes: they are often the same". More than two-thirds of that demand comes from the country's rural population. Gold is the second largest import item for India after petroleum. Over 90% of the gold consumed in India is imported. A French visitor to India, Francois Bernier, enviously wrote how "It should not escape notice that gold and silver, after circulating in every other quarter of the globe, come at length to be absorbed in Hindustan."[6]

The performance of gold in Indian rupees certainly confirms that gold for Indians is an excellent hedge against inflation and devaluation of their fiat currency. Gold has, since 2000, increased close to ten times in rupee terms and, even after the recent drop, it is still seven times higher than its 2000 level. In 2009, the government of India purchased 200 metric ton of gold from the International Monetary Fund (IMF) at $6.7 billion. This purchase has propelled the India Bullion Market to the tenth position among the top global gold holders.

This purchase signals that the economy of the country has come full circle and is also a way of spreading its assets. The current foreign exchange or forex reserve of India is nearly $285 billion. The share of foreign currency in the forex is $268.3 billion, followed by gold at $10.3 billion, IMFs special drawing rights accounts for $5.2 billion while the reserve position in the IMF accounts for $1.59 billion.

The Reserve Bank of India, in July 2013, had imposed severe restrictions on gold imports in order to check the burgeoning current account deficit and sliding rupee, which led to a decline in official demand for gold of 26% to 190.3 tonnes during the January-March 2014 quarter. However, acts of smuggling precious gold into the country have multiplied alarmingly ever since the government imposed tight restrictions on gold imports, a year ago.

---

[6] Commoditytrade.com: Role of India in the Global Gold Market, Access date between April 10, 2014 to April 12, 2014, from https://goldprice.org/gold-price-chart.html

There has been a sharp rise in cases of gold smuggling across all airports in the country. Singapore, Sri Lanka and the Middle East countries are the key sources from where gold in huge quantities are smuggled to India by air. Gold premiums in India confirm that the demand for gold has not been curtailed much by the restriction; it only boosted black market demand. India gold premiums have more than doubled since the restrictions were implemented, and they recently halved on hopes of easier import rules.

IBMA or the Indian Bullion Market Association is a national level body that represents the Indian Bullion Trade and Industry. This body is an association of all leading bullion dealers and jewelry merchants who have tied up with the National Spot Exchange Limited. The idea of this association is to promote a professional organizational dedication towards the development and growth of the bullion industry in India.

Indian Bullion Market Association (IBMA) is the national level body being set-up to represent the Indian bullion trade and industry. It is a consortium of leading bullion dealers and jewellery merchants of India, who have joined hands with National Spot Exchange Limited, the pan India Electronic Spot Market for commodities. The idea is to promote a professional organization dedicated towards the growth and development of bullion trade and industry. IBMA is committed to identify the inefficiencies involved in Indian bullion market and to create a momentum to remove such inefficiencies in a gradual but steady manner.[7]

India is the leading consumer and importer of bullion. It consumes nearly 800 MT of gold, which accounts for 20 per cent of world gold consumption. Out of this, around 600 MT of gold goes into making jewellery. The domestic bullion and jewellery market is estimated to be around US$ 16.1 billion, which is expected to grow to the size of US$25 billion within 2-3 years. India's gem & jewellery sector commands around 80% of the jewellery trade worldwide. Total Export of jewellery in April 2009 was at Rs.5749.56 Crore.

[7] Indian Bullion Market, Access date between February 10, 2014 to February 13, 2014, from http://www.ibma.co.in/indian_bullion.htm

There are a number of restrictions imposed on the import and export of gold as compared to any other commodities. The bullion market of the country is very fragmented and unorganized. The price of bullion varies very much in different parts of the country. The main reason for this is the lack of a benchmark that is valid throughout the country.

Graph No. 1.1

Graph shows the countries with largest Gold Reserve

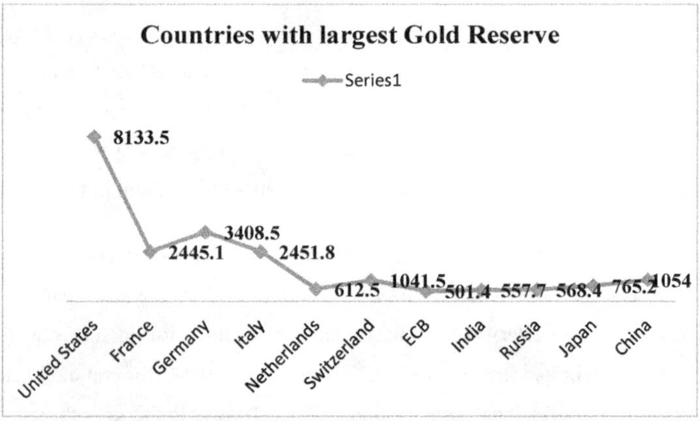

Source: http://www.usfunds.com/investor-library

India has always been a significant player in the international gold market and had a thriving bullion spot and futures market till the enactment of the Gold Control Act in 1963 which debarred the general public from holding or trading in gold. Since 1990, the government has been taking a number of steps to reform this sector and ensure that India benefits from the demand influence it has on the gold business internationally.

The liberalization of the gold sector has been in stages; first allowing a number of banks to import gold – braking the monopoly of the State Trading Corporations; then considerably reducing the import duty – destroying a lucrative parallel smuggling channel and now allowing traders, manufacturers as well as investors to trade in gold futures in India itself.

Since the liberalization of the gold market in India, Indians buy on an average of about 600 tonnes or Rs 40,000 crores worth of gold every year in the form of jewellery &

investments. In addition, another 200 tonnes of gold passes through the hands of the Indian jeweller for conversion into new pieces of jewellery. India, USA, Middle East, Japan, China account for 55 percent of the global gold consumption.[8]

Gold is currently at crossroads. There is a growing interest in gold as an alternative to mainstream financial assets. By no means all investors are convinced that the US and World economies are in sustainable recovery mode. Some of the most astute international financial managers are turning to gold, as well as other currencies and commodities, as top investments while inflation picks up and the dollar deteriorates in value. Low short-term interest rates mean holding cash is an unattractive option and hence supporting investments in alternate assets. Finally, the international political environment continues to create a great deal of anxiety. This suggests the external factors will remain supportive for gold investment. The supply side is expected to remain fairly inelastic because new mine supply has long gestation periods and the de-hedging of gold by the produces is expected to continue.

Gold sales by the Reserve Banks of various countries, is also expected to remain regulated within the Central Bank Gold agreement. Hence the critical factor in the supply side of the equation will be the re-sale of above the ground stockpile of gold held by household in countries such as India, Middle East and some of the South East Asian countries. Price spikes in 2002 and the first quarter of 2003 –during the Iraq war- had resulted in increasing supply of old gold into the Indian & Middle East markets, however such price related disinvestments behaviour has been absent during the recent price spiral in November/December 2003. One of the strengths of gold as an Asset class is that its price is not determined by the performance of any company or economy and there is significant above the ground stocks - estimated at 147,800 tonnes (present market value Rs 88,68,000 crores) hence the gold prices move in a more orderly fashion as compared to any other commodity or financial asset.

---

[8]Frank Holmes (2016): Countries with Largest Gold Reserves, Access date between April 8, 2015 to April 12, 2015, from http://www.usfunds.com/investor-library

1.5 OBJECTIVES OF BULLION MARKET

The main objectives of Bullion Market are as follows:

1. Bullion Market provides an effective, professionally managed, legally compliant solution for owning physical gold with minimal counterparty risks, global diversification options, access to commercial liquidity sources and multiple exit strategies.

2. Serve as a strategic reserve that is uncorrelated to financial assets and could provide access to global liquid buying power, with no haircut, when it matters the most.

3. Keep 100% of net assets invested in gold bullion at all times.

4. Offer the ability to custom-tailor geographic diversification through access to insured private, non-bank vaults including Switzerland, Dubai, Singapore, Hong Kong and the U.S.

5. Ensure safe custody and investor protections by maintaining strong control environment and compliance procedures that overlay a robust ownership structure.

6. Employ experienced, professional managers that can evaluate the changing regulatory, economic and political landscape and adapt to contingencies.

7. Establish and maintain relationships across a global network of bullion dealers, refiners, secure logistics services and vaulting facilities.

8. Bullion markets exist across the globe and most of the transactions take place through electronic means or by phone.

9. The versatile uses of silver and gold in many areas especially its industrial applications decide the prices of the precious metal.

10. Bullions are considered as a safe bet to hedge against inflation or as a safe haven for investment.

1.6 HISTORY OF BULLION

Bullion has a cornerstone of Human civilization for centuries. Bullion undoubtedly represented an insurance policy against an uncertain future, a currency with universal value when all else fails. Bullion is the ultimate reserve.

Claude de Bullion, became the French Minister of Finance in 1632 under King Louis XIII. He was an extremely rich man and so great was his cash pile, extensive property holdings and business interests that the generic term of 'Bullion,' emerged after his name and which came to symbolize untold wealth. Monsieur Bullion was not a popular man in France and when he died, he was obliged to be buried at night time to avoid a baying mob. Even a hundred years later his reputation for excessive wealth had not diminished and during the French Revolution his tomb was sacked and destroyed.

Gold has been traded for over two thousand years, and in particular, the Spanish traded gold and silver captured from their conquests in South America during the middle ages. So the trading of precious metals on the open market is nothing new, and now as in the past, their value is based on the purity, mass and weight of the commodities being marketed. These metals could be in the form of coins, ingots and bars.

The purity of gold is defined by using a centuries old technique of fire essay (you can see essay marks on gold and silver bars, ingots and silver which provide origin, date and help value the item). Today, this old methodology is combined with a modern spectroscopic instrumentation to ensure perfect accuracy. The European Union regulates the purity of gold bullion (99.5% for gold bars) and (90% for bullion coins).

The world's trade in bullion is based in London and their standards are considered to be the benchmark for quality and safe delivery of gold and silver bars whatever their origin. The Bullion Market is where the wholesale trading of gold and silver is undertaken. The London Bullion Market Association coordinates the activities of its members and other market participants and promotes quality standards and fineness to ensure that gold bars traded are 99.5% pure and silver is 99.9%. This regulated trading ensures that standards are maintained and fairness prevails for buyers and sellers wherever they are located.

You don't need to buy whole gold bars and ingots to be a precious metal investor. Items like gold and silver Britannia coins, gold Sovereigns, PAMP (Swiss made 100 gram gold bars), 22 carat gold Krugger and coins, American Eagle gold coins and small Metalor silver bars and many other objects in platinum and palladium (a very fine white platinum often used in rings) can be purchased through organizations like The Gold Bullion Company in Birmingham.

Bullion is often a good hedge against currency risks, inflation worries and other geopolitical uncertainties and of course any sound investor likes to have a portfolio with a spread of investment channels.

The Gold Bullion Company, based in the heart of Birmingham's old jewellery quarter, buys and sells gold coins, silver bullion and silver coins from many of the world's leading precious metal mints, including The Royal Mint, and overseas mints, Metalor and Umicore. We feature a wide range of bullion products that can be purchased on-line from as little as less than twenty pounds up to many thousands. Once an order has been placed, The Gold Bullion Company securely posts the fully insured item(s) direct to the buyer.

Since the financial market crash of 2008 the banks and building societies have offered a very poor return on investments; with continuing low interest rates, many saver/investors have chosen alternative and more lucrative outlets to place their investments. One of these has been bullion. As with any financial decision you need to be absolutely confident of the organisation in which you are planning to place an investment. Buying bullion will be for many people a first-time experience and perhaps slightly daunting but it doesn't have to be. The Gold Bullion Company has over eight thousand five hundred customers and a 99.6% satisfied customer rating.

Buyers can purchase a gold bar for less than £100 or invest in a collection of Royal Mint Silver Coins costing several thousand pounds. As a long established family firm, the Gold Bullion Company has gained a sound reputation for honest, straightforward business dealings and prides themselves on the quality of their unbiased, pre and post sales advice. The Company's customer care team will advise buyers on the most suitable investment product for them and every purchase made comes with a buy-back guarantee. During the British Raj bullion of gold and silver were imported into India through ships. Mumbai, then called Bombay, was one of the major hubs for bullion trade in India. The market was full of traders and jewellers. The bullion era as fondly call it, was the glittering era for the traders. Dated back in 1919, the seed was sowed for the formal association of the bullion traders. This was the inception of the famous Bombay Bullion Association (BBA). In 1920 the forwards market of bullion in Bombay (now Mumbai) was one of the largest in the world. Dated on 24 January, 1923, the BBE, Bombay Bullion Exchange ltd. was registered as an organisation which gradually grew to facilitate the traders with a safety vault. Change and growth both are a part of nature. So happened with the bullion organisation, it gradually grew into various departments from Melting and Refining to Assaying, from Dharam Kanta to Bullion ring and forward trading. Over the years it was registered in the consciousness of the traders of the market and became famous as The Bombay Bullion Association Ltd. growing to the pinnacles of being the apex body for bullion trade in India. The Bombay Bullion Association worked for pan India operations.

The Apex association of India the BBA still gives the opening and closing rates of bullion across India. Even RBI follows the rates given by the association. The scientific approach adopted by the association for assaying can only be challenged by the government body 'the Mint'. This association has being the pride of the traders and members associated with it. Independent India Post-independence India was confronted with many challenges; the transition phase when Indian trade and the people began to assert their presence with all things "Indian" also gave rise to anarchy and confusion amidst the business communities, with the bullion industry being one of them. Comprehending the need to establish an unbiased and neutral organization which could use a multi-faceted approach in not only facilitate the working of an structured business sector but also address disputes and act as the conciliator between dealers, provide a neutral and correct platform for weighing precious metals acceptable to the trading community, interact with different governmental and executive agencies, provide reliable and correct reports of assaying of precious metals acceptable to the parties involved, the association was formed.

The Bombay bullion Association Ltd. established in September 1948, today is associated with more than 50,000 members actively involved and participating in its activities. After independence in 1947, the government of India gave its recognition to The Bombay Bullion Association Ltd and asks all the small bullion association existing in Bombay to merge with the association. Later in 1948, it was declared that, Bombay Bullion association Ltd was the guarantee and the association company and not the company with share capital. As envisaged since its establishment, the Bombay Bullion Association Ltd. has proved to be an unbiased platform that has received wide acceptance amongst the entire precious metal trading community.

1.7 TYPES OF BULLION

Various types of bullion are as follows:

A. Bullion Coins

Bullion Coins are the physical precious metal in a coin shape. Its value is almost entirely derived from its melt value alone. By definition a bullion coin is struck by a sovereign government mint. They almost always have an enforceable legal tender face value.

A bullion coin is a coin struck from precious metal and kept as a store of value or an investment rather than used in day-to-day commerce. A bullion coin is distinguished by an explicit statement of weight (or mass) and fineness on the coin; this is because the weight and composition of coins intended for legal tender is specified in the coinage laws of the issuing nation, and therefore there is no need for an explicit statement on the coins themselves. The United Kingdom defines investment coins more specifically as coins that have been minted after 1800, have a purity of not less than 900 thousandths and are, or have been, legal tender in their country of origin. Under United States law, "coins" that fail the last of these requirements are not coins at all, and must be advertised as "rounds" instead. The American Eagle and Canadian Gold Maple Leaf series are the only coins available in gold, silver, platinum, and palladium.

Bullion coins are typically available in various weights. These are usually multiples or fractions of 1 troy ounce, but some bullion coins are produced in very limited quantities in kilograms or heavier. Bullion coins sell for a premium over the market price of the metal on the commodities exchanges. Reasons include their comparative small size and the costs associated with manufacture, storage and distribution. The amount of the premium varies depending on the coin's type and weight and the precious metal. The premium also is affected by prevailing demand.

The ISO currency code for gold bullion is XAU. ISO 4217 includes codes not only for currencies, but also for precious metals (gold, silver, palladium and platinum, by definition expressed per one troy ounce, as compared to "1 USD") and certain other entities used in international finance, e.g. special drawing rights.

1. Gold Coins

The largest demand for gold in the world is jewelry, which consumes 50% of world production. Industry uses 9%, coins use 10% and the rest is for investments. Starting in

1821, with Britain moving to the gold standard, countries monetary unit became associated with the value of circulating gold or stored gold bullion, but not both. During this time, gold coins were circulated for general use. During the early years of the Great Depression, nations dropped the gold standard and most gold coins were no longer minted. The South African Krugger and became the first modern coin minted in 1967 to help market South African gold produced by Rand Refinery and the South African Mint. By 1980, the Krugerr and accounted for 90% of the global gold coin production.

Gold Coins in India

Gold is something that many Indians buy during festivals such as Akshaya Tritiya, Dhanteras . Other than jewellery, we buy physical gold in the form of bars and coins. Many prefer to buy gold coins over jewellery as the former can be bought in denominations low as 0.5 grams. If you too are planning on buying gold coins this festive season, here are 7 things that you must keep in mind.

Gold Coins in India

(i) Purity of gold coins

There are two ways to measure the purity of gold coins - Karat and fineness. Karat is the more commonly used measure of gold purity. 24 Karat (KT) is considered to be purest form of gold which contains 24/24 parts of gold. Similarly, 22KT gold contains 22 parts of gold and 2 parts of other metals such as zinc or silver to make it more durable while making jewellery.

Fineness is another parameter used to measure the purity of gold and is mainly to find the purity of 24KT gold. As per the World Gold Council's website, even 'pure' gold can contain minute amounts of mixed impurities which the manufacturer has not been able to remove. Fineness is defined as weight of precious metal (such as gold) in proportion to the total weight (which includes alloy and impurities). It is expressed in units of parts per 1,000. The purest form of gold, i.e., 24KT, when measured in fineness shows 999.9 parts per thousand of purity.

(ii) Hallmarking

While buying a gold coin apart from purity, one should also check if it is hallmarked. Government of India has set up the Bureau of Indian Standards (BIS) to ensure that consumers are not cheated while buying gold. BIS certifies gold and silver coins and jewellery by stamping it (embossing its mark on the gold item) to certify the level of purity of the item.

(iii) Packaging

It is advisable that one must buy gold coins in a tamper proof packaging. The packaging is a guard against counterfeiting, fraud, and damage, explains Sinha. Jewellers recommend that one should not tear or open the tamper proof packaging of the gold coin in case one intends to resell it, as the packing ensures the credibility of the purity of the gold coin.

(iv) Denominations

Usually, gold coins are available in the market ranging from 0.5 grams to 50 grams in weight. So, going by current price of Rs 31,447 (as on May 3, 2019 on the Multi

Commodity Exchange), the smallest gold coin you could buy, i.e., of 0.5 gms, should cost between Rs 1500 to Rs 1600 for 24KT coin (without making charges and taxes, as on May 3, 2019. However, availability of the denomination you wish to buy depends on the jeweller.

(v) Making charges

Buying gold coins is relatively easier as compared to jewellery. It offers you the option to buy the purest form of gold in the minimum weight of 0.5 grams with lower making charges in comparison to ornaments like earrings, rings etc. Making (or manufacturing) charges for gold coins usually ranges between 8 percent and 16 percent, says Sinha. On the other hand, making charges for jewellery generally starts from 8 percent and can go higher depending on the craftsmanship.

(vi) Options to buy from

Apart from the local jeweller, one can also buy gold coins from online e-tailers, banks, the Stock Holding Corporation of India, MMTC (a government-authorised public sector unit for the sale of gold and silver), and certain non-banking financial companies like the Muthoot Group.

However, the minimum denomination of gold coins will vary from one entity to another. Only a few like the Muthoot Group offer smaller denomination coins in 0.5 grams. According to Muthoot's website, it offers gold coins starting from as low as 0.5 grams of 24 KT/ 999 fineness. Muthoot also offers coins with different designs like that of Lakshmi, Ganesha etc., and the lowest denomination varies according to design.

Banks like Canara Bank offer 24KT gold in denomination of 5 grams, 8 grams and 10 grams as mentioned on their website. Stock Holding Corporation offers gold coins of 24 KT/999 fineness in partnership with MMTC with a starting denomination of one gram.

(vii) Ease of selling

If you have bought gold coins or are planning to buy from a bank, do keep in mind that they will not buy back those coins as per a Reserve Bank of India (RBI) directive.

2. Palladium

Palladium is a silvery-white metal. Its primary uses are for catalytic converters, jewelry, electronics, professional flutes and fuel cells. The highest price for an ounce of palladium was $1,600 in 2019.

Palladium is a chemical element with the symbol Pd and atomic number 46. It is a rare and lustrous silvery-white metal discovered in 1803 by William Hyde Wollaston. He named it after the asteroid Pallas, which was itself named after the epithet of the Greek goddess Athena, acquired by her when she slew Pallas. Palladium, platinum, rhodium, ruthenium, iridium and osmium form a group of elements referred to as the platinum group metals (PGMs). These have similar chemical properties, but palladium has the lowest melting point and is the least dense of them.

More than half the supply of palladium and its congener platinum is used in catalytic converters, which convert as much as 90% of the harmful gases in automobile exhaust (hydrocarbons, carbon monoxide, and nitrogen dioxide) into less noxious substances (nitrogen, carbon dioxide and water vapor). Palladium is also used in electronics, dentistry, medicine, hydrogen purification, chemical applications, groundwater treatment, and jewelry. Palladium is a key component of fuel cells, which react hydrogen with oxygen to produce electricity, heat, and water.

Ore deposits of palladium and other PGMs are rare. The most extensive deposits have been found in the norite belt of the Bushveld Igneous Complex covering the Transvaal Basin in South Africa; the Stillwater Complex in Montana, United States; the Sudbury Basin and Thunder Bay District of Ontario, Canada; the Norilsk Complex in Russia and most recently, the northern part of the Visayas islands in the Philippines.[4] Recycling is also a source, mostly from scrapped catalytic converters. The numerous applications and limited supply sources result in considerable investment interest.

Characteristics

Palladium belongs to group 10 in the periodic table, but the configuration in the outermost electrons is in accordance with Hund's rule. Electrons in the s-shell migrate to fill the d orbitals because they have less energy.

Palladium is a soft silver-white metal that resembles platinum. It is the least dense and has the lowest melting point of the platinum group metals. It is soft and ductile when annealed and is greatly increased in strength and hardness when cold-worked. Palladium dissolves slowly in concentrated nitric acid, in hot, concentrated sulfuric acid, and when finely ground, in hydrochloric acid. Palladium does not react with oxygen at standard temperature (and thus does not tarnish in air). Palladium heated to 800 °C will produce a layer of palladium (II) oxide (PdO). It tarnishes lightly in a moist atmosphere containing sulfur.

3. Platinum

Platinum is a silverish-white with its name is derived from the Spanish term platino, meaning "little silver". Platinum is used in catalytic converters, electronics and jewelry. The first and only case when platinum coins were used as a regular national currency was in Russia. The coins were minted between 1828 and 1845. Russia stopped minting platinum coins as it proved to be impractical: platinum resembles many less expensive metals, and, unlike the more malleable and ductile silver and gold, it is very difficult to work. From 1975 to 1985, the Isle of Man sold commemorative coins with various designs such as a gyrfalcon, herring, Manx cat, and of the Manx Loaghtan sheep. The American Platinum Eagle comes in two versions. The bullion version is a static design while the proof versions are the only U.S. bullion coins that change designs every year. The highest price for platinum was $2250 an ounce in 2008.

Platinum is a chemical element with the symbol Pt and atomic number 78. It is a dense, malleable, ductile, highly unreactive, precious, silverish-white transition metal. Its name is derived from the Spanish term platino, meaning "little silver".

Platinum is a member of the platinum group of elements and group 10 of the periodic table of elements. It has six naturally occurring isotopes. It is one of the rarer elements in Earth's crust, with an average abundance of approximately 5 μg/kg. It occurs in some nickel and copper ores along with some native deposits, mostly in South Africa, which accounts for 80% of the world production. Because of its scarcity in Earth's crust, only a few hundred tonnes are produced annually, and given its important uses, it is highly valuable and is a major precious metal commodity.

Platinum is one of the least reactive metals. It has remarkable resistance to corrosion, even at high temperatures, and is therefore considered a noble metal. Consequently, platinum is often found chemically uncombined as native platinum. Because it occurs naturally in the alluvial sands of various rivers, it was first used by pre-Columbian South American natives to produce artifacts. It was referenced in European writings as early as 16th century, but it was not until Antonio de Ulloa published a report on a new metal of Colombian origin in 1748 that it began to be investigated by scientists.

Platinum is used in catalytic converters, laboratory equipment, electrical contacts and electrodes, platinum resistance thermometers, dentistry equipment, and jewelry. Being a heavy metal, it leads to health problems upon exposure to its salts; but due to its corrosion resistance, metallic platinum has not been linked to adverse health effects.[6] Compounds containing platinum, such as cisplatin, oxaliplatin and carboplatin, are applied in chemotherapy against certain types of cancer.

4. Rhodium

Rhodium is a rare silver-white metallic element. Its primary use is in catalytic converters found in automobiles. The highest price for Rhodium was in 2008 when it rose above $10,000 per ounce ($350,000 per kilogram). The first and only coin produced is Tuvalu's South Sea Dragon. There have been two bars produced by Pamp and Baird & Co.

Rhodium is a chemical element with the symbol Rh and atomic number 45. It is a rare, silvery-white, hard, corrosion-resistant, and chemically inert transition metal. It is a noble metal and a member of the platinum group. It has only one naturally occurring isotope, 103Rh. Naturally occurring rhodium is usually found as free metal, alloyed with similar metals, and rarely as a chemical compound in minerals such as bowieite and rhodplumsite. It is one of the rarest and most valuable precious metals.

Rhodium Coins

Rhodium is found in platinum or nickel ores together with the other members of the platinum group metals. It was discovered in 1803 by William Hyde Wollaston in one such ore, and named for the rose color of one of its chlorine compounds.

The element's major use (approximately 80% of world rhodium production) is as one of the catalysts in the three-way catalytic converters in automobiles. Because rhodium metal is inert against corrosion and most aggressive chemicals, and because of its rarity, rhodium is usually alloyed with platinum or palladium and applied in high-temperature and corrosion-resistive coatings. White gold is often plated with a thin rhodium layer to improve its appearance while sterling silver is often rhodium-plated for tarnish resistance. Rhodium is sometimes used to cure silicones, a two part silicone where one part contains a silicon hydride and the other containing a vinyl terminated silicone are mixed. One of these liquids contains a rhodium complex. Rhodium detectors are used in nuclear reactors to measure the neutron flux level. Other uses of rhodium include asymmetric hydrogenation used to form drug precursors and the processes for the production of Roundup and acetic acid.

5. Silver Coins

The first modern silver bullion coin was the Mexican Onza. It was minted in 1949 and struck intermittently with that date until the 1978, 1979 and 1980 mintages. Mexico created a new coin, the Libertad, in 1982. It was not released until 1984 due to a financial crisis in Mexico. The value of the coin is listed as 1 Onza. The Libertad and South Korea's ZI:SIN are technically not bullion coins as they are not legal tender. In 1986, the American Eagle became the second bullion coin to be minted.

Silver Coins

It was authorized by the Title II of Public Law 99-61 (Liberty Coin Act) as a way to reduce America's stockpiled silver and to pay for the federal budget. In its first year, 5.8 million Silver Eagle coins were minted. The most minted in one year occurred in 2015, with 47.9 million coins. Countries that did not have their own mints, turned to private mints. Majority of these coins are done for Pacific or Caribbean island nations and are used to bring income into their treasury. Examples are Congo's silverback gorilla coin minted by Scottsdale Mint and Niue's hawksbill turtle minted by New Zealand Mint.

B. Bullion Rounds

Bullion Rounds are the physical precious metal in a flat round or wafer shape. Its value is almost entirely derived from its melt value alone. By definition a bullion round is struck by private mint.

Rounds are minted by private mints and have no face value. They're not intended to ever circulate as currency. As an investment in metals, rounds are great stores of value since their value is based solely off its Precious Metal content. This usually means that it is more affordable to buy Silver rounds than Silver coins, or Gold rounds than Gold coins, especially rare coins.

Designs for rounds are limitless, often commemorating events and stories or honoring favored interests like sports, wildlife, holidays and even comic book characters. Many rounds pay homage to historical coins, and are designed as almost exact replicas. The Hobby Protection Act of 1973 requires that imitation rounds, and other numismatics, be clearly marked with "COPY" to quickly identify replicas and prevent fraud.

Another interesting difference between coins and rounds that prevents counterfeiting: rounds cannot be made with the exact dimension and weight of any coin produced anywhere in the world. This allows for some interesting size listings including everything from 1/25 oz Gold rounds to 1/4 oz Copper rounds to 1 oz Silver rounds.

C. Bullion Bars

Bullion Bars are the physical precious metal in a bar or ingot form. Its value is almost entirely derived from its melt value alone. Mostly struck by private mints, although some sovereign mints (like the Royal Canadian Mint for example) strike bullion bars.

Indians have been big consumers of gold. People own physical gold in the form of jewellery, gold coins, and even gold bars.

Nowadays, in addition to purchasing gold from your neighbourhood jeweller, you can buy it from e-commerce websites such as Amazon, Snapdeal, and Flipkart.

Compared to gold coins and jewellery, bars can come at a lesser cost. However, there are a few things you should consider before you buy them. Read on to find out what they are.

1. Purity: Make sure what you want is what you get. Ensure that the gold you are buying is pure. Karat is the unit used to measure the purity of gold, higher the karat, more pure the gold is. Therefore, 24, 22, 18 karat gold has the purest form in that order. In case of 24k gold, all 24 parts in the gold are pure gold with extremely low level of impurities. If you are purchasing for investment purpose, 24K suits else opt for 22K if you intend to use it for your own consumption. The price of 24K is higher than lower karat gold.

2. Refinery: While purchasing, it helps to know the refinery from where the gold bar has been refined. Purchasing gold bars which have been refined at popular refineries ensures highest level purity. Bangalore Refinery and MMTC-PAMP (a joint venture between public sector MMTC and Switzerland's PAMP SA) are two such refineries in India.

3. Tolerance level: Ask about the weight and purity tolerance level (variation in purity) while purchasing. Some gold bars may have a +/- tolerance levels while some bars may come with NIL negative weight tolerance and NIL negative purity tolerance, thus assuring that the customer always receives right value for what is paid for.

4. Fineness: Fineness shows the purity of precious metals by parts per thousand rather than karats. Fineness is another way of expressing the precious metal content of gold jewellery, and represents the purity in parts per thousand. When gold is refined to a fineness level of 999.9 parts per thousand it is stated as 999.9.

5. Denomination: Choosing to invest in lower denominations helps to maintain liquidity when you need it. Opt for gold bars with lower denominations. The denomination of gold bars can be as low as 5gm and also available in 10g, 50g, 100g even up to 1 kg. The price of higher denomination may, however, be less as it commands lesser premium.

6. Certification: The benchmark to follow while buying gold online is to look for Hallmark certification. It is imperative for you to ensure that the gold you buy is from a BIS (Bureau of Indian Standards) Hallmarked jeweller. And the ornament/coin/bar carries BIS hallmark. There's a list of jewellers selling BIS-certified jewellery on the BIS website

7. Packaging: If the gold bar is packaged as is the case when you buy it online, don't take it out of the packaging. Keeping the packaging intact helps in maintaining the purity of the gold bar.

8. Return policy: Always check for the website or seller's return or buyback policy while buying gold online. These days most big gold chains have their online stores and they

offer both returns and exchange. However, the exchange policy of gold has stricter terms and conditions as compared to other items sold online. So, it is important to go through the terms and conditions carefully before making your purchase decision.

Types of Gold Bar – The Cast Gold Bar

Cast gold bars are made in a similar method to ingots of gold. The molten metal is poured into a bar-shaped mould. It is then left to solidify as it returns to room temperature. The mould is then removed from the gold brick.

This process can cause malformed bars with uneven surfaces, however, it is unlikely to be too much of an issue for its use as a source of wealth, as the bullion will still need to conform to weight and purity measures. If the bullion bar does not meet these requirements, it is typically melted down again and its raw material used in the next production cycle.

Types of Gold Bar – The Minted Gold Bar

The minted gold bar is made in a completely different way. It is cut from a block of gold, in much the same way as you would produce a coin. This minting process uses a series of dies to create the size and texture of the gold bullion bars and the associated embossed lettering. The weight of the bar is maintained, and the bar itself will possess the shiny lustre that is wanted by most personal investors, particularly those people who are giving gold as a gift.

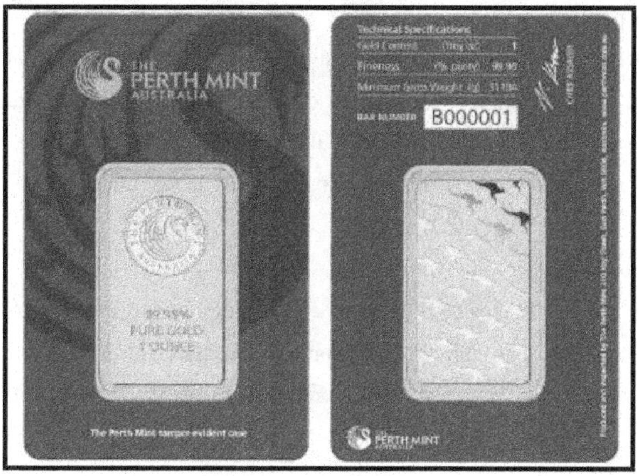

1.8 ADVANTAGES OF BULLION MARKET

With the consideration of various research articles, experts and scholars, the following advantages of bullion market were identified:

1. Inflation Hedge

Gold and silver are precious metals that have been used as a medium of trade for thousands of years. In contemporary society, gold and silver are no longer used as a form of money, but some people still like to own bullion as a tangible source of wealth to offset the vagaries of inflation. The idea is that while the purchasing power of the dollar has steadily declined, the purchasing power of gold and silver has remained stable.[9]

2. Inherent Value

Investors who are bullish on gold, known as "gold bugs," assert that paper money has no inherent value beyond that ascribed to it by the government. Gold and silver are tangible assets which have inherent value based in part on their industrial uses and in part on their scarcity. While the government can print up as many dollars as it wishes, there is only so much gold and silver available in the world.[9]

3. Tangible Asset

One can gain exposure to gold and silver by investing in precious metals exchange traded funds, gold and silver mutual funds or the stocks of precious metals mining companies. However, owning gold or silver bullion gives you access to the physical investment. Bullion is available in small size coins, bars and ingots that can be easily stored in a home safe or bank safe deposit box.

4. Considerations

There are advantages to buying gold and silver bullion as a portion of your diversified investment portfolio, but there are some considerations to be aware of before you take the plunge. Not all gold and silver bullion is created equal.

Gold and silver bullion comes in different levels of fineness, or purity. Some bullion coins contain different percentages of the precious metal than others. For example, American Eagle gold bullion coins are .9167 fine, or 22 karat, while Vienna Philharmonic bullion coins have a fineness of .9999, or 24 karats. The Federal Trade Commission advises investigating both the bullion and the seller before you invest in gold or silver bullion.

5. Price is Less Volatile Compared to Other Assets

There is more than one reason why people prefer to go with gold as compare to other investment solutions. The gold market has the record of staying high for a long period of time. Be it any country of the world, the gold markets touches the peak and continues to stay there for a long period of time which is why people consider it to be the best way of preserving their wealth.

6. Globally Accepted

Gold is acceptable all over the world. Moreover, there is certainly no different type of gold in different parts of the world which mean you can trade it regardless of your locations. You can simply keep the gold with you and sell it whenever you get perfect rates for it.

---

[9]Mike Parker (2014). Advantages of Buying Gold or Silver Bullion, Access date between May 10, 2016 to May 13, 2016, from https://budgeting.thenest.com

1.9 DRAWBACKS OF BULLION MARKET

Bullion markets are not free from several drawbacks. With the consideration of various research articles, experts and scholars, the following disadvantages of bullion market were identified:

1. Liquidity

Gold is a wonderful long-term investment, but it is not the best way to store your funds in the short-term. When you are buying physical gold, you are buying it from a dealer, which means paying slightly over the market price of gold at the time. And the process is the same if you want to sell gold, and dealers usually pay a little less than the market price when they are buying your gold, because they consider it their commission. So if you are in a rush to sell your gold, you may have to put up with getting less money for your investment than the going market rate. It is why you should most definitely not put all your savings in gold, because you can never know when an emergency situation may require you to liquidate some of your assets. But if you put roughly 10 or 20 percent of your long-term savings in physical gold, the lack of liquidity should not pose any issues for you.[10]

2. No Broker Assistance

The fact that brokers often advice against gold investments stems from the fact that they are not allowed to deal in physical gold. If you are getting all your investment money managed by a broker or through a brokerage, it is a little inconvenient to have to find a separate dealer for gold. In addition, your broker may not have the necessary knowledge or expertise about gold to advise you on how much to buy, or where to buy it from. But if you are willing to do the leg work on finding reputable dealers of gold, the process of buying gold is fairly straightforward. A vast majority of gold dealers are in it for the long haul, which means you may only have to deal with one or two gold dealers in your lifetime.

3. Political Climate

Like any other investment, gold is impacted by the political situation in the world at any given moment. There are particular areas in the world where gold mining is especially lucrative, and any political strife in those regions may impact the price of gold temporarily. In addition, concerns about whether a central bank or national government may sell a large portion of their gold supply can prompt fears that the price of gold is about to crash. However, fears of price fluctuation exist in every single investment you could make. Even the money sitting in your bank account or in your drawer could instantly lose a ton of its value depending on inflation rates. Investors who have studied the history of gold investments know that any price fluctuations you see with gold, especially a decline in its price, are only temporary.

If you are investing in gold for the long-term, a one or two-year dip in its price is not going to impact you in any way. The price will eventually stabilize, and as history has shown us, will inevitably rise from one decade to another.

4. Minimal Gains amidst Market Stability

One of the benefits to gold investment is how it hedges against a market collapse. But in the same vein, gold prices usually do not display significant gains during periods of market stability or progress. When investors have a great deal of confidence in the financial markets, they are less likely to put their money in gold, which means the supply of gold in the world increases, which can either drive down prices or keep them at a stable level. While you are very unlikely to lose money on a gold investment over a ten or twenty-year period, if the said period coincides with a time where the markets perform very well, your investment may not produce as great a return as you were expecting.

5. Not Regular Profit

People usually with lack of knowledge and invest in gold but sooner or later they realize that investing in gold isn't bringing much advantage to them. Buying gold and keeping it with you isn't going to bring any benefit at all, not unless you decide to sell it. There is no interest or income you are getting out of that gold.

---

[10]Sneha B K (2015). Disadvantages of Investing in Gold, Access date between July 20, 2016 to July 25, 2016, from https://www.goodreturns.in/personal-finance

6. Commissions

If you are investing in gold by buying in form of jewels then you might end up paying a lot of commission to the seller in the name of the making of the jewellery.

7. Non-Predictable Gold Market

Moreover, if you check the history of the gold and its prices, you will realize that despite the fact that the prices of gold stays high for a long period of time, there are times when the prices out of nowhere starts dropping which is not at all a good thing for the investor. There are very less chances of one making any profit out of gold investments. However, if it is a part of your portfolio it may not hurt you as it will get balanced with other assets.

8. Not very healthy profit

As long as you are willing to remain patient with your gold investment, by the time you do sell your gold, you are going to make a very healthy profit in relation to the price you paid to buy it. Even if your dealer of choice gives you less than the market rate at the time of selling, the market rate is probably going to be so much higher than it was when you bought the gold, which means a profit is all but guaranteed.

1.10 KEY ROLES OF BULLION MARKET

Some key insights from the report are highlighted below:

1. Demand responds more to income than it does to price. Our econometric analysis of data from 1990 to 2015 revealed that income levels are the most significant long-term determinants of consumer gold demand: holding all else equal, a 1% rise in income boosts gold demand by 1%.

2. Income is the most powerful factor, and income levels are expected to rise. The IMF has forecast per capita GDP to grow by 35% for 2015–2020 and the National Council of Applied Economic Research expects India's middle class to double, exceeding 500 million (m) by 2025.

3. The report states that, valued at over US$800bn, India's gold stocks are around 23,000-24,000 tonnes. Southern India has the highest market share for gold demand of 40%,

Western India at 25% and Northern and Eastern India have 20% and 15% of the market share respectively.

4. Gold jewellery plays a dual role in India - as an investment as well as an adornment, hence a considerable number of Indians invest in gold through 22k jewellery. Given that weddings are a key occasion for buying gold and the fact that 500m of the population is under the age of 25, the number of weddings and subsequently the occasions for buying gold are likely to be higher. The outlook for jewellery demand is favourable.

5. We estimate there are between 385,000 and 410,000 jewellers in India. The majority – around 70% – of India's jewellery industry can be categorised as unorganised. Between 2000 and 2015 more organised participants emerged, with their market share rising from 5% to 30%. By 2020, it is likely that this share will have risen to between 35% and 40%. For many investors, bars and coins are considered a safe investment and rank alongside deposit accounts as a preferred savings vehicle. By 2020, the report indicates that, bar and coin demand will be between 250–300 tonnes.

6. Consumers prefer to pledge jewellery or bullion as collateral to raise funds rather than selling them. Around 1,250 tonnes is used as collateral, largely with informal lenders, such as pawnbrokers. The report states that gold loans will continue to hold a bigger market share in India. Owing to the government's encouragement to the formal sector, money-lenders and pawnbrokers, will lose market share to banks and gold loan companies.

7. India is reliant on imports and recycling to meet gold demand. Gold imports account for around 85% of total supply, and the refining sector plays an important role in taking these imports and putting them in a form suitable for India's gold industry. Indian gold refining capacity jumped in recent years from mere three or four refineries in 2013 to 30 in 2015, taking the total capacity above 1,450t.

8. India is one of the largest gold jewellery exporters in the world. In FY2015–2016, Indian gold jewellery shipments came to US$8.6bn.

1.11 INVESTMENTS IN BULLION

Many analysts are agreed that being invested in commodities, including precious metals, is a good thing. Most confine their recommendations to funds that invest in a basket of commodities. However although a rise in gold spot selling prices improves the fortunes of a gold mining company, it probably faces challenges from declining output and increasing costs; so that its share price does not tally with the way that gold bullion rises in price due to its increasing scarcity. And other investment classes like property, oil & gas etc. are often included in the fund and can distort fund performance, limiting your exposure to the actual bullion market.

Nearer to the market are 'paper gold' certificates and 'ETCs' which purport to grant you ownership of the real asset: but the definition of ownership can be cloudy and you need to understand what these concepts actually involve.

Buy and sell of Bullions

The investors can buy physical bullion in a range of countries. However this can bring with it tax charges and you need to compare the advantages of different locations when thinking of how to buy gold, including those offshore. It is important to invest with a supplier that has a transparent, liquid market for buying back bullion at favourable rates that do not disadvantage the holder. Suppliers like Bullion Rock offer a transparent selling process that is simple and advantageous. Beware of offers of 'all-in-one' pricing where you cannot relate the deal to market rates.

You will often discover that companies who sell bullion to you, particularly in the case of bars, will discount the market price by only 2% or 2.5% if you bought it from them: but bars that you have bought elsewhere may be penalized by a 4% cost (suppliers will factor in the possible requirement for them to re-assay your bars to restore their status to the prime 'good delivery' category).

Investment in Bullion in the form of Jewellery

Indians certainly cherish possessing gold. But owning it in the form of jewellery has its own concerns about safety, high costs, and outdated designs. Then there are the 'making charges', which could prove to be a costly affair. The making charges on gold jewellery, which typically ranges between 6 percent and 14 percent of the cost of gold (may go as high as 25 percent in case of special designs) are irrecoverable.

Gold Coin Scheme

Gold coins can be bought from jewellers, banks, non-banking finance companies, and now even e-commerce websites. The government has launched ingeniously minted coins which will have the National Emblem of Ashok Chakra engraved on one side and Mahatma Gandhi on the other. The coins are available in denominations of 5 and 10 grams while the bars will be for 20 grams.

The Indian Gold Coin and Bar will be of 24 karat purity and 999 fineness carrying advanced anti-counterfeit features and tamper proof packaging. All coins and bars will be hallmarked as per the BIS standards. These coins are distributed through designated and recognised MMTC outlets and through specified bank branches and post offices. MMTC also offers a transparent 'buy back' option for Indian Gold Coin through its own showrooms across India. MMTC will repurchase the Indian Gold Coin, in intact tamper proof packaging and with original invoice, at the prevailing gold base rate.

Gold savings schemes

Gold or jewellery savings schemes come in two forms. A typical one allows you to deposit a fixed amount every month for the chosen tenure. When the term ends, you can buy gold (from the same jeweller) at a value that is equivalent to the total money deposited, including a bonus amount. This conversion is done at the gold price prevailing on maturity. In most cases, the jeweller adds a month's instalment at the end of the tenure as a cash incentive or may even offer a gift item.

Gold exchange traded funds (ETF)

An alternate way of owning paper gold in a more cost-effective manner is through gold exchange traded funds (Gold ETF). Such investments (buying and selling) happens on a stock exchange (NSE or BSE) with gold as the underlying asset. What's more, the high initial buying and even selling charges that go into owning jewellery, bars or coins gives an extra edge to the low-cost gold ETF. The transparency in pricing is another advantage. The price at which it is bought is probably the closest to the actual price of gold and therefore the benchmark is the physical gold price.

What you need is a trading account with a stock broker and a demat account. One may either buy in lump sum or even at regular intervals through systematic investment plans (SIP). You may even buy 1 gram of gold.

Even though there are no entry or exit charges there are three costs that come with gold ETFs. One is the expense ratio (for managing the fund) which is generally low compared to other mutual funds and is around 1 percent. Second, is the broker cost that needs to be accounted for every time you buy or sell gold ETF units. Third, which technically is not a charge but impact returns is the tracking error. It arises because of the fund's expenses and cash holdings thus not mirroring actual gold price.

Sovereign Gold Bonds (SGB)

Sovereign Gold Bond is another way of owning paper gold. They are issued by the government but availability is not 'on-tap basis'. Instead, the government will intermittently open a window for the fresh sale of SGBs to investors. This could typically happen every 2-3 months and the window will remain open for about a week. For investors looking to purchase SGBs anytime in between the only way out is to buy earlier issues (at market value) which are listed in the secondary market.

Investment in Digital Gold

You can now purchase gold coins, bars and jewellery online. 'Digital Gold', is offered on the mobile wallet platform of Paytm and 'GoldRush' is offered by the Stock Holding Corporation of India on their website, while Motilal Oswal has launched Me-Gold, a digital gold online investment. All of these are offered in association with MMTC - PAMP, (a joint venture between public sector MMTC and Switzerland's PAMP SA)

The initial cost of owning physical gold in the form of bars or coins is anywhere around 10 percent and it is even higher for jewellery. SGB and Gold ETF, both paper-gold, are cost effective as there is no entry cost in SGB while costing for gold ETF could be around 1 percent.

SGB should benefit those who want to invest in gold for a longer period as its maturity is after 8 years, although the lock-in ends from the fifth year. However, gold ETF provides much better liquidity than SGB. Owing units is much easier than SGB as it's entirely online in case of ETFs. The risk of owning, holding also doesn't exist in both.

The big difference is on the taxation front. Gains in SGB on redemption are tax-exempt but gains in Gold ETFs after 3 years are subject to 20 percent tax post indexation.

Also, the only disadvantage with gold ETFs is that its units won't be earn the additional interest of 2.5 per cent per annum like you would get for SGBs.

Get clarity as to why you need to invest in gold - is it for marriage purpose or for pure investment. For investments, one should not have more than 10 percent of the total portfolio in gold. Choose between Gold ETFs or SGBs depending on how comfortable you are managing investments online and keep the worries of purity, security aside.

1.12 RISKS OF INVESTING IN BULLION MARKETS

An investment in physical precious metal at Gold offers a form of wealth insurance and an opportunity to realize good returns; however, it also entails risks and is therefore not suitable for every investor. It is important that you gain a good understanding of the characteristics and risks of investing in physical precious metal before you take an investment decision. In addition, you should also carefully consider whether an investment in physical precious metal is suitable for you in view of your experience, investment horizon, other investments, financial position, risk appetite and other relevant circumstances.

1. Price Risk

The price development of precious metal depends on the movements in the market. As a result, the value of precious metal can fluctuate and the price of your precious metal can be lower than the price for which you purchased it. If the value of your precious metal drops to zero, you could even lose the value of your whole investment. The price of the precious metal at the time that you enter an order via your account and issue it to Gold is not necessarily the price at which the order shall be executed as a delay in the execution can occur. This applies in particular - but not exclusively - to orders that are placed outside of business days.

2. Exchange Rate Risk

Worldwide, the value of precious metal is expressed and traded in US dollars. As you purchase your precious metal in euros, the value or your investment is influenced by exchange rate effects. An appreciation of the US dollar versus the euro has a positive effect, whereas depreciation has a negative effect.

3. Bankruptcy of Bank

Cash that you maintain in your cash depot is held via SBDG at the Rabobank in The Netherlands or ING DiBa in Germany. Both well reputed banks with a high, stable creditworthiness. Nevertheless, these banks could go bankrupt or experience financial problems as a result of which you can lose (part of) your money. SBDG is not a bank and is not subject to the deposit guarantee system.

4. Trading Interruptions

Due to special circumstances it can occur that trading is not possible and as a result physical precious metal cannot be purchased or sold via Gold. After trading is resumed, the prices can differ from the prices that were issued before the trading interruption. Gold (computer) system, website, the Internet, etc., could be (temporarily) inaccessible or your own computer could malfunction. As a result, it is possible that you are unable to carry out a transaction or unable to carry out a transaction at the desired time or at the desired price.

5. Operational Risk

This is the risk that due to a shortcoming in the working of the procedures of Gold errors are not observed timely or fraud could even occur. Gold aims to counter this by means of a sound division of tasks, a well-documented administration organization and supervision of the compliance with the agreed procedures.

6. Identity Theft

If your password does not remain confidential and is obtained by a third party, you run the risk that a third party can gain access to your account. In principle, this third party can only carry out transaction or transfer your cash to your contra account. As it is not possible to transfer cash to another account. The risk that you run is therefore: a violation of your privacy and the placing of ghost orders. The first matter is a nuisance; but the second matter can also lead to losses due to price differences.

7. Insurance Exclusions

Gold ensures that your precious metals are adequately insured against theft and damage. Exclusions apply to each insurance policy. If exclusion occurs as a result of which no insurance payment follows, Gold is not liable for the damage. The cover that the insurance offers is specified in the insurance policies that are published on the Gold.

8. Laws and Regulations

Amendments to the applicable laws and regulations can be implemented, government measures can be announced or new interpretations of the supervisor of investments can be published that can have consequences for the business operations of Gold and can also lead to an increase of the rates for buying and selling transactions via Gold.

1.13 RATIONALE OF THE STUDY

Investment is not free from risk and if the investment in bullion market this is absolutely true. Risk is an important component in assessment of the prospects of an investment. Most investors while making an investment consider less risk as favorable. The lesser the investment risk, more lucrative is the investment. However, the thumb rule is the higher the risk, the better the return.

Because of high level of investment risk in bullion market, there is a need for identifying parallel options for reducing those investment risks. The present study purely dedicated to identifying best way of investment especially in Gold. Like most commodities, the price of gold is driven by supply and demand, including speculative demand. However, unlike most other commodities, saving and disposal play larger roles in affecting its price than its consumption. Most of the gold ever mined still exists in accessible form, such as bullion and mass-produced jewelry, with little value over its fine weight so it is nearly as liquid as bullion, and can come back onto the gold market. The present study was relevant to understand the dimensions of Gold Futures and probable risks with special reference to bullion market that guides the new investors.

Hence to conclude, this chapter covers the concept significance of bullion market. Also and how the Indian bullion market is recognizable index that highlight the economic growth. History, Objectives and advantages and drawbacks along with the key roles of bullion market is being covered under this chapter.

CHAPTER - 2

HEDGING AND RISK MANAGEMENT

Hedging deals with reducing the risk of uncertainty related to the adverse price fluctuations in an asset. Hedging is not used to make profits but rather to prevent or at least minimize possible losses. The futures exchange is commonly used to hedge against price risks. Market participants obtain derivatives on the exchange to cover themselves against price movements. These futures contracts and options on these exchanges are rarely executed. The position will be offset, which means obtaining an opposite contract to settle the contract. The commodity will then be sold on the cash market and the profit or loss made by offsetting the futures position will be added to the final cash price. The possible profit or loss is then covered by the profit or loss made by the futures contract. The various types of risks associated with investing in bullion market are market risk, default risk, Inflation risk, interest rate risk, financial risk, political risk, liquidity risk and emotional risk. The market mood is influenced by the political climate in the country. Combating all these types of risks is a major challenge. The bullion market can be a great thing, but both the buyers and sellers to the future contract must first understand the risks and their risk tolerance before putting their money to work in the market. A hedge is an investment that protects your finances from a risky situation. Hedging is done to minimize or offset the chance that your assets will lose value. It also limits your loss to a known amount if the asset does lose value. It's similar to home insurance. You pay a fixed amount each month. If a fire wipes out all the value of your home, your loss is only known amount of the deductible.[11]

2.1 DESCRIBE THE CONCEPT HEDGING

Hedging is an insurance method for commodity traders, producers and end-users to cover themselves against negative price movements. The aim of this strategy is to restrict the losses that may arise due to unknown fluctuations in the investment prices and to lock the profits therein. It works on the principle of offsetting i.e. taking an opposite and equal position in two different markets.

[11]Kimberly Amadeo (2016). Hedging and How It Works, Access date between February 10, 2014 to February 15, 2014, from https://www.thebalance.com

In simple terms, it is hedging one investment by investing in some other investment. Generally, when people plan to hedge, they try to insure themselves against a negative event. This does not prevent the event from occurring, but it surely reduces its impact. Not only individual investors but portfolio managers and large corporations also use this hedging technique to minimize the exposure to various types of risks and decrease the negative impact thereon. Hedging techniques generally involve the use of complicated financial instruments known as derivatives, the two most common of which are options and futures. This is not going to get into the nitty-gritty of describing how these instruments work, just keep in mind that with these instruments can develop trading strategies where a loss in one investment is offset by a gain in a derivative.

Hedging is a risk management strategy which is used in limiting or offsetting probability of loss from fluctuations in the prices of commodities, currencies, or securities. Hedging is done to minimize the chance of lose value. It also limits the loss to a known amount if the asset does lose value.[12]

2.2 AREAS OF HEDGING AND THEIR RISKS

A business can implement hedging technique in the following areas:

1. Commodities

Commodities include agricultural products, energy products, metals, etc. The risk associated with these commodities is known as "Commodity Risk". The commodities market works just like any other market. It is a physical or a virtual space, where one can buy, sell or trade various commodities at current or future date. One can also do commodity trading using futures contracts. A futures contract is an agreement between the buyer and the seller, wherein the buyer promises to pay the agreed-upon sum at the moment of the transaction when the seller delivers the commodity at a pre-decided date in the future. A farmer can thus buy wheat futures to fix a price at which he would want to sell a certain amount in future. Similarly, a trader might buy or sell wheat futures for delivery on a future date at a price decided now.

---

[12]Waspi, Kevin G. (2012). Financial Markets: A Practicum. Great River Technologies. pp. 349–359.

India has six commodity exchanges Multi Commodity Exchange (MCX), National Commodities and Derivatives Exchange (NCDEX), National Multi Commodity Exchange, Indian Commodity Exchange, ACE Derivatives Exchange and the Universal Commodity Exchange.

2. Securities

Securities include investments in shares, equities, indices, etc. The risk associated with these securities is known as "Equity Risk" or "Securities Risk". Brokers sell securities and commodities directly to individual clients. They advise people on appropriate investments based on the client's needs and financial ability. The people they advise may have very different levels of expertise in financial matters. Finding clients is a large part of a broker's job. They must create their own client base by calling from a list of potential clients. Some agents network by joining social groups, and others may rely on referrals from satisfied clients. Investment bankers connect businesses that need money to finance their operations or expansion plans with investors who are interested in providing that funding. This process is called underwriting, and it is the main function of investment banks. The banks first sell their advisory services to help companies issue new stocks or bonds, and then the banks sell the issued securities to investors. Some of the most important services that investment bankers provide are initial public offerings (IPOs), and mergers and acquisitions. An IPO is the process by which a company becomes open for public investment by issuing its first stock. Investment bankers must estimate how much the company is worth and ensure that it meets the legal requirements to become publicly traded. Investment bankers also connect companies in mergers (when two companies join together) and acquisitions (when one company buys another). Investment bankers provide advice throughout the process to ensure that the transaction goes smoothly.

3. Currencies

Currencies include foreign currencies. There are various types of risks associated with it. For e.g. "Currency Risk (or Foreign Exchange (Currency) Exposure Risk)", "Volatility Risk", etc. Managing currency risk began to capture attention in the 1990s in response to the 1994 Latin American crisis, when many countries in that region held foreign debt that exceeded their earning power and ability to repay, and the 1997 Asian currency crisis, which started with the financial collapse of the Thai baht. Currency risk can be reduced by hedging, which offsets currency fluctuations. If a U.S. investor holds stocks in Canada, the realized return is affected by both the change in stock prices and the change in value of the Canadian dollar against the U.S. dollar. If a 15% return on Canadian stocks is realized and the Canadian dollar depreciates 15% against the U.S. dollar, the investor breaks even, minus associated trading costs. Many exchange-traded funds (ETFs) and mutual funds are designed to reduce currency risk by being currency hedged, typically using options and futures. The rise in the U.S. dollar has seen a plethora of currency-hedged funds introduced for both developed and emerging markets such as Germany, Japan and China. The downside of currency-hedged funds is that they can reduce gains and are more expensive than funds that aren't currency-hedged. Black Rock's iShares, for example, has its own line of currency-hedged ETFs as an alternative to its less-expensive flagship international funds. In early 2016, investors began reducing their exposure to currency-hedged ETFs in response to a weakening U.S. dollar, a trend that's since continued and has led to the closures of a number of such funds.[13]

4. Interest Rates

Interest rates include the lending and borrowing rates. The risks associated with these rates are known as "Interest Rate Risks". The Reserve Bank of India increased its key policy repo rate by 25bps to 6.5 percent on August 1st 2018, in line with market expectations and following a similar hike in the previous meeting. Policymakers reinforced that the decision is consistent with a neutral monetary policy stance and is in line with achieving the inflation target of 4 percent +/- 2 percent while supporting growth. The reverse repo rate was also adjusted to 6.25 percent from 6 percent and the marginal standing facility rate and the Bank Rate to 6.75 percent from 6.5 percent. Interest Rate in India averaged 6.66 percent from 2000 until 2018, reaching an all-time high of 14.50 percent in August of 2000 and a record low of 4.25 percent in April of 2009.

[13]Jorion, Philippe (2009). Financial Risk Manager Handbook. John Wiley and Sons. p. 287-188.

2.3 CLASSIFICATION OF HEDGING

Not only for reducing risk, hedging is also useful as a means to earn profits by trading in various commodities, securities or currencies. Depending on these areas, broadly there are three types of hedging:

1. Forward

Forward (or a Forward Contract) is a non-standardized contract to buy or sell an asset between two independent parties at an agreed price and a specified date. It covers various contracts like Forward exchange contracts for currencies, commodities, etc. The price of the underlying instrument, in whatever form, is paid before control of the instrument changes. This is one of the many forms of buy/sell orders where the time and date of trade is not the same as the value date where the securities themselves are exchanged.[14]

Forwards, like other derivative securities, can be used to hedge risk (typically currency or exchange rate risk), as a means of speculation, or to allow a party to take advantage of a quality of the underlying instrument which is time-sensitive. A closely related contract is a futures contract; they differ in certain respects. Forward contracts are very similar to futures contracts, except they are not exchange-traded, or defined on standardized assets. Forwards also typically have no interim partial settlements or "true-ups" in margin requirements like futures – such that the parties do not exchange additional property securing the party at gain and the entire unrealized gain or loss builds up while the contract is open. However, being traded over the counter (OTC), forward contracts specification can be customized and may include mark-to-market and daily margin calls. Hence, a forward contract arrangement might call for the loss party to pledge collateral or additional collateral to better secure the party at gain. In other words, the terms of the forward contract will determine the collateral calls based upon certain "trigger" events relevant to a particular counterparty such as among other things, credit ratings, value of assets under management or redemptions over a specific time frame, e.g., quarterly, annually, etc.

---

[14]Pope, Geoff (2010). "Foreword" Versus "Forward"". Grammar Girl's Quick and Dirty Tips. Macmillan Holdings, LLC. Retrieved 10 August 2015.

2. Futures

Futures are a standardized contract to buy or sell an asset between two independent parties at an agreed price, standardized quantity, and a specific date. It covers various contracts like currency futures contracts, etc. Futures contracts are standardized for quality and quantity to facilitate trading on a futures exchange. The buyer of a futures contract is taking on the obligation to buy the underlying asset when the futures contract expires. The seller of the futures contract is taking on the obligation to provide the underlying asset at the expiration date. Futures contracts are used by two categories of market participants: hedgers and speculators. Producers or purchasers of an underlying asset hedge or guarantee the price at which the commodity is sold or purchased, while portfolio managers and traders may also make a bet on the price movements of an underlying asset using futures. An oil producer needs to sell their oil. This way they can lock in a price they will sell at, and then deliver the oil to the buyer when the futures contract expires. Similarly, a manufacturing company may need oil for making widgets. Since they like to plan ahead and always have oil coming in each month, they too may use futures contracts. This way they know in advance the price they will pay for oil (the futures contract price) and they know they will be taking delivery of the oil once the contract expires. Futures are available on many different types of assets. There are futures contracts on stock exchange indexes, commodities, and currencies. Imagine an oil producer plans to produce one million barrels of oil over the next year. It will be ready for delivery in 12 months. Assume the current price is $75 per barrel. The producer could produce the oil, and then sell it at the current market prices one year from today. Given the volatility of oil prices, the market price at that time could be very different than the current price.

3. Money Markets

Money market refers to a section of the financial market where financial instruments with high liquidity and short-term maturities are traded. It is one of the major components of financial markets today, where short-term lending, borrowing, buying and selling are done with the maturity of one year or less. Money markets cover a variety of contracts like money market operations for currencies, money market operations for interest, covered calls on equities, etc.

Money Market Instruments

In this market, only those financial instruments are traded which are immediate substitutes for money, which includes:

(i) Call/Notice Money: When the money raised or borrowed on demand for a very short term which ranges from one day to 14 days, then it may be called as notice money, and when it exceeds 14 days it is termed as call money.

(ii) Treasury Bills: These are short term, negotiable financial assets issued by the central bank, on behalf of the government, for overcoming liquidity shortfalls.

(iii) Commercial Bills: A commercial bill is a negotiable, self-liquidating instrument that is less risky in nature. When goods are bought on credit, these bills improve the liability to make payment at the specified date.

(iv) Commercial Paper: It alludes to an unsecured promissory note, issued by large and creditworthy companies, at a discount on its face value and redeemable at its face value.

(v) Certificate of Deposit: It is an unsecured, negotiable financial instrument which a bank and financial institution issues to individuals, corporation, trust, funds etc. at a discount on its face value and its maturity vary from 15 days to one year. The financial assets dealt in the money market possess high liquidity, low transaction cost, less risky and no loss in value. And so, it acts as a whole sale debt market for such instruments.

2.4 HEDGING STRATEGIES

A hedging strategy generally refers to the risk reduction technique of an investment. There can be no standard strategy to hedge various financial instruments like forward contracts, options, swaps or stocks because these strategies require constant modification as per the type of market and investment, which requires hedging. To face such situations, a business can implement few strategies which are as follows:

1. Hedging Through Asset Allocation

You can do this by diversifying your portfolio with more than one type of asset. For e.g. you can invest 70% in equity and the rest 30% in other more stable assets, to create a balanced portfolio.

2. Hedging Through Structures

You can do this by investing a portion of the portfolio in debt and the other in derivatives. Where debt portion brings stability to the portfolio, the derivatives help in protecting it from the downside risk.

3. Hedging Through Options

You can do this by buying a call option and selling a put option and vice-versa. This helps directly in protecting the portfolio, especially the equity portfolio.

4. Staying In Cash

It is a 'No Investment' strategy. Here, the investor does not make an investment in any asset and thereby keeps his cash in hand.

2.5 GOLD HEDGE FUND MANAGER

The hedge fund manager and the investment team are possibly the key element for the fund's success. It is the final touch of the manager and the analysts that matters when applying various strategies. Because of that, the manager should have considerable knowledge in the area of portfolio management, and also in several other crucial departments, including but not limited to economics and finance. A gold hedge fund manager will also have to have knowledge specific to the precious metals market. This would encompass the knowledge of what possibly drives the prices of precious metals and other market-specific factors.

While the strategy of a hedge fund gives you the general idea what kind of returns and risk you might expect (this is never precise, though), in the end it's the fund manager who decides on all the details of the strategy and its implementation. Examples of this, specific to gold hedge funds, would include answering questions such as:

1. What kinds of precious metals are owned by the fund?
2. Does the fund own only paper gold and silver or is there a significant share of securities representing real metals?
3. Does the fund invest in senior mining stocks or juniors, or both?
4. Does the fund implement geographical diversification?
5. Does the fund utilize sector-specific rebalancing techniques?

It is the manager that answers these questions and comes up with specific trading and investment ideas. As always, much focus is put on the track record of a given manager and investors might choose to gravitate to managers who have outperformed the buy-and-hold approach over a relatively long period of time. Having said that, you have to remember that past performance is not a guarantee of future returns and that trading and investment always involves risk, even with the best of managers.

2.6 GOLD HEDGE FUND PERFORMANCE

The performance of a gold fund depends on the general performance of the precious metals market (fundamental situation for the precious metals) but also on the fund manager and their strategy. The intuitive measure of how well the fund manages money is its long-term performance. The history of the fund returns and their variability is one of the main considerations here. You have to remember, however, that the past performance of the fund doesn't guarantee that it will enjoy the same kind of returns in the future as the market might be more unpredictable than one might think.

The typical hedge fund cost structure is called "2 and 20" which means that the fund charges 2% annually on the assets of the fund (annual management fee) and 20% of the profits that the fund generated (performance fee). These costs weigh in on the after-fees performance of the fund. In choosing a gold fund, you have to assess whether the fund adds value in the sense that it's able to improve the risk-return characteristics of your investment or that it gives you peace of mind which you hold dear. The annual management fee is charged to ensure that the fund is able to cover various operating costs such as the costs of setting up a fund, legally required fees, software licenses and various other costs.

Gold Hedge Fund in India

Gold Fund is a mutual fund or ETF (Exchange-Traded Fund) that invests predominantly in gold bullion or gold-producing companies. In case the fund invests primarily in bullion, or in stocks and bonds of gold manufacturers and miners, the price of the shares within these funds will majorly correlate to the spot price of gold. The objective of this fund is to get returns from gold investments in a convenient way.

Gold funds can be an ideal investment tool for anyone who wishes to protect their capital against inflation or political instabilities. Gold funds can be of different types and they have been briefly explained below:

i) Gold ETFs - The underlying asset in these type of funds is physical gold and hence, its value is dependant on the price of gold. Gold ETFs are ideal for investors who wish to invest in physical gold but do not want the hassle of storing or securing the gold against theft. A demat account is a must to invest in Gold ETFs.

ii) Gold Mining Funds - These funds do not invest in physical gold but instead make investments in companies that are involved in the mining of gold. The returns from these funds depend on the performance of these gold mining companies.

iii) Gold Fund of Fund - These funds make investments in the units of Gold ETF and investors do not require a demat account to invest in its units.

Benefits of Investing in a Gold Fund

Important Benefits of Investing in a Gold Fund are as follows:

a) Investing in Gold Mutual Funds gives investors the benefit of exposure to the gold asset in an easy way.
b) Investors can invest in the precious metal without having a Demat Account.
c) Units of gold funds can be bought and sold at any time during business hours and from any part of the country due to which GST will not apply for the difference in the gold price.
d) Investors can reap the benefits of the potential value of gold without actually possessing tangible gold.
e) Gold funds can be used as a hedge against geopolitical instabilities and inflation.
f) It is a convenient way to diversify your investment portfolio.
g) It is a safe investment option as gold rates do not witness fluctuations too often.
h) Gold ETFs allow easy trading through a stock broker or a fund manager.
i) As there is no entry or exit system for buying the units of gold funds, they are very economical.
j) Gold is a good investment as a bet against a falling currency.

k) Gold funds that have been subscribed to for more than a year can reap capital gains over the long term. These funds also do not attract wealth tax or securities transaction tax.

l) You can use gold ETFs as a collateral while borrowing money from a bank or a financial institution.

m) Since each unit of gold ETFs are backed by pure gold prices, there is no risk to the purity.

List of Gold Funds in India

i) Growth Gold Mutual Funds - The growth option of gold funds will help investors achieve capital gains at the end of the investment period.

ii) Dividend Gold Mutual Funds - The dividend option will offer regular income to the investor in the form of dividends. The dividends can be given out as payouts or can be reinvested back to the scheme.

Some of the top gold funds in India have been given below:

a) Axis Gold Fund
b) Aditya Birla Sun Life Gold Fund
c) Canara Robeco Gold Savings Fund
d) HDFC Gold Fund
e) ICICI Pru Regular Gold Savings Fund
f) IDBI Gold Fund
g) Invesco India Gold Fund
h) Kotak Gold Fund
i) Quantum Gold Saving Fund
j) Reliance Gold Savings Fund
k) SBI Gold Fund

2.7 ADVANTAGES OF HEDGING

Following are the various advantages of Hedging:

a) Futures and options are very good short-term risk-minimizing strategy for long-term traders and investors.

b) Hedging tools can also be used for locking the profit.

c) Hedging enables traders to survive hard market periods.

d) Successful hedging gives the trader protection against commodity price changes, inflation, currency exchange rate changes, interest rate changes, etc.

e) Hedging can also save time as the long-term trader is not required to monitor/adjust his portfolio with daily market volatility.

f) Hedging using options provide the trader an opportunity to practice complex options trading strategies to maximize his return.

2.8 DISADVANTAGES OF HEDGING

Following are the disadvantages of Hedging

a) Hedging involves cost that can eat up the profit.

b) Risk and reward are often proportional to one other; thus reducing risk means reducing profits.

c) For most short-term traders, e.g.: for a day trader, hedging is a difficult strategy to follow.

d) If the market is performing well or moving sidewise, then hedging offer little benefits.

e) Trading of options or futures often demand higher account requirements like more capital or balance.

f) Hedging is a precise trading strategy and successful hedging requires good trading skills and experience.

2.9 DESCRIBE THE CONCEPT OF RISK

Risk is the potential that a chosen action or activity including the choice of effective which will lead to a loss an undesirable outcome. The idea implies that a choice having an influence on the outcome exists. Potential losses themselves may also be called risks. Risk is a combination of five primitives: outcome, likelihood, significance, causal scenario and population affected.[15]

[15]Kumamoto and Henley (2015). International Conference in Applied Protection and Its Trends, Online Journal of Applied Knowledge Management, 3(3). pp-19-25

The concept risk starts with a risk-oriented approach to social security by defining its basic objective as the provision of people with the resources to cope with specified common risks in life. Furthermore social security schemes protect society against collective risks associated with poverty, epidemics, marginalization, crime, etc.

The conception of social security as an insurance provides an approach to social policy that is different from that of social assistance and income redistribution. On a global level, this approach also embodies specific views about the essential content of the welfare society and its internal logic, highlighted by the concept of the global village, i.e. civil society, rather than simply the concepts of global markets and the global network of states.

All investments carry some degree of risk. The rule of thumb is the higher the risk, the higher the potential return, but the need to consider an addition to the rule so that it states the relationship more clearly, the higher the risk, the higher the potential return and the less likely it will achieve the higher return. A fundamental idea in finance is the relationship between risk and return. The reason for this is that investors need to be compensated for taking on additional risk.

Every instrumental method, such as insurance, adopted in social policy formulation, has a specific logical relationship to certain normative value structures in society which will be reinforced by that method, but also to a particular substantive target problem, with the intention to influence this by the same method within the framework of accepted values in society.

The term discourse refer to structured thinking, reasoning, speaking or writing on social security, based on this systemic interdependence and interaction between substantial, instrumental and normative aspects. Thus, discourse is not merely an academic concept in textual analysis but a practical vehicle for political communication and, consequently, policy formulation.

Much of the debate on the welfare state, especially among economists, has concentrated on its effects on consumption, labour supply and economic growth, expressing the well-known dichotomy in opinion between proponents and opponents towards social security.

It does not intend to enter into this debate here, since it focuses on economic performance and consumption levels rather than on social security and general welfare.

The economic debate on the welfare state often does not recognize risk protection as a substantive element, neither as an individual value nor as a social benefit or a public good. Consequently it also fails to see the difference between measures aimed at risk protection and measures aimed at income redistribution.

Large welfare states do factually exist, and draw substantial political support in many, if not even most, developed countries. The main question and challenge is how best to organize them, by which premises, and according to what discourse.

Social security benefits could be understood rather strictly as measures aimed at providing security against different risks. The concept of security implies insurance in the true meaning of this concept and not simply social assistance or income redistribution.

Examples: Currency risk, inflation risk, principal risk, country risk, economic risk, mortgage risk, liquidity risk, market risk, opportunity risk, income risk, interest rate risk, prepayment risk, credit risk, unsystematic risk, call risk, business risk, counterparty risk, purchasing-power risk, event risk.

Meaning of Risk

Risk is the probability or threat of damage, injury, liability, loss, or any other negative occurrence that is caused by external or internal vulnerabilities, and that may be avoided through preemptive action. A hedge is a risk management technique used to reduce any substantial losses or gains suffered by an individual or an organization.

Definition of Risk

According to Hansson and Sven Ove, "Risk is the potential of losing something of value, weighed against the potential to gain something of value. Values such as physical health, social status, emotional well-being or financial wealth can be gained or lost when taking risk resulting from a given action, activity and/or inaction, foreseen or unforeseen".[16]

---

[16]Sven Ove Hansson (born 1951). "Dimensions of risk". Risk Analysis. 9 (1): 107–112.

2.10 PRINCIPLES OF RISK

The several principles of risk are as follows:

i) Managerial Context: An organization may be immune to change in import duty whereas a different organization operating in the same industry and environment may be at a severe risk. There are also marked differences in communication channels, internal culture and risk management procedures. The risk management should therefore be able to add value and be an integral part of the organizational process.

ii) Participation of Stakeholders: The risk management process should involve the stakeholders at each and every step of decision making. They should remain aware of even the smallest decision made. It is further in the interest of the organization to understand the role the stakeholders can play at each step.

iii) Organizational goals: When dealing with a risk it is important to keep the organizational objectives in mind. The risk management process should explicitly address the uncertainty. This calls for being systematic and structured and keeping the big picture in mind.

iv) Reporting: In risk management communication is the key. The authenticity of the information has to be ascertained. Decisions should be made on best available information and there should be transparency and visibility regarding the same.

v) Roles and Responsibilities: Risk Management has to be transparent and inclusive. It should take into account the human factors and ensure that each one knows it roles at each stage of the risk management process.

vi) Maintain Structure: Structure underlines the importance of the risk management team. The team members have to be dynamic, diligent and responsive to change. Each and every member should understand his intervention at each stage of the project management lifecycle.

vii) Caution Indicators: Keep track of early signs of a risk translating into an active problem. This is achieved through continual communication by one and all at each level. It is also important to enable and empower each to deal with the threat at his/her level.

viii) Reconsider sequence: Keep evaluating inputs at each step of the risk management process - Identify, assess, respond and review. The observations are markedly different in each cycle. Identify reasonable interventions and remove unnecessary ones.

2.11 CLASSIFICATION OF RISK

The various types of risks are as follows:

i) Financial Risk

It is the risk borne by equity holders due to a firm's use of debt. If the company raises capital by borrowing money, it must pay back this money at some future date plus the financing charges. This increases the degree of uncertainty about the company because it must have enough income to pay back this amount at some time in the future.

ii) Static and Dynamic Risks:

A second important distinction is between static and dynamic risks. Dynamic risks are those resulting from changes in the economy. Changes in the price level, consumer tastes, income and output, and technology may cause financial loss to members of the economy. These dynamic risks normally benefit society over the long run, since they are the result of adjustments to misallocation of resources. Although these dynamic risks may affect a large number of individuals, they are generally considered less predictable than static risks, since they do not occur with any precise degree of regularity.

Static risks involve those losses that would occur even if there were no changes in the economy. If we could hold consumer tastes, output and income, and the level of technology constant, some individuals would still suffer financial loss. These losses arise from causes other than the changes in the economy, such as the perils of nature and the dishonesty of other individuals. Unlike dynamic risks, static risks are not a source of gain to society. Static losses involve either the destruction of the asset or a change in its possession as a result of dishonesty or human failure. Static losses tend to occur with a degree of regularity over time and, as a result, are generally predictable. Because they are predictable, static risks are more suited to treatment by insurance than are dynamic risks.

iii) Fundamental and Particular Risks

The distinction between fundamental and particular risks is based on the difference in the origin and consequences of the losses. Fundamental risks involve losses that are impersonal in origin and consequence. They are group risks, caused for the most part by economic, social, and political phenomena, although they may also result from physical occurrences. They affect large segments or even all of the population. Particular risks involve losses that arise out of individual events and are felt by individuals rather than by the entire group. They may be static or dynamic. Unemployment, war, inflation, earthquakes, and floods are all fundamental risks. The burning of a house and the robbery of a bank are particular risks. Since fundamental risks are caused by conditions more or less beyond the control of the individuals who suffer the losses and since they are not the fault of anyone in particular, it is held that society rather than the individual has a responsibility to deal with them. Although some fundamental risks are dealt with through private insurance, usually, some form of social insurance or government transfer program is used to deal with fundamental risks. Unemployment and occupational disabilities are fundamental risks treated through social insurance. Flood damage or earthquakes make a district a disaster area eligible for federal funds.

In the final analysis, whether a risk is considered fundamental or particular depends on current public opinion concerning the responsibility for the causes and consequences of the risk. In the aftermath of the terrorist attack on the World Trade Centre on September 11, 2001, congress and the insurance industry debated the question of whether terrorist attacks are a fundamental or particular risk. Reinsurers- the insurers that provide insurance to insurance companies- announced their intent to exclude acts of terrorism from the coverage they provide to other insurers. Faced with the loss of backup coverage, the insurers that deal with the public developed an endorsement for their policies excluding loss from terrorist acts. In response to these developments, congress considered several bills to create a federal terrorism reinsurance program but by March 2002 had reached an impasse regarding the form that such a program should take.

Particular risks are considered to be the individual's own responsibility, inappropriate subjects for action by society as a whole. They are dealt with by the individual through the use of insurance, loss prevention, or some other technique.

iv) Pure and Speculative Risks

One of the most useful distinctions is that between pure risk speculative risk. Speculative risk describes a situation in which there is a possibility of loss, but also a possibility of gain. Gambling is a good example of a speculative risk. In a gambling situation, risk is deliberately created in the hope of gain. The student wagering Rs.10 on the outcome of Saturday's game faces the possibility of loss, but this is accompanied by the possibility of gain. The entrepreneur or capitalist faces speculative risk in the quest for profit. The investment made may be lost if the product is not accepted by the market at a price sufficient to cover costs, but this risk is borne in return for the possibility of profit. The term pure risk, in contrast, is used to designate those situations that involve only the chance of loss or no loss. One of the best examples of pure risk is the possibility of loss surrounding the ownership of property. The person who buys an automobile, for example, immediately faces the possibility that something may happen to damage or destroy the automobile. The possible outcomes are loss or no loss.

The distinction between pure and speculative risks is an important one, because normally only pure risks are insurable. Insurance is not concerned with the protection of individuals against those losses arising out of speculative risks. Speculative risk is voluntarily accepted because of its two-dimensional nature, which includes the possibility of gain. Not all pure risks are insurable, and a further distinction between insurable and uninsurable pure risks may also be made.

v) Personal risks

Personal risks consist of the possibility of loss of income or assets as a result of the loss of the ability to earn income. In general, earning power is subject to four perils: (a) premature death, (b) dependent old age, (c) sickness or disability, and (d) unemployment.

vi) Property risks

Anyone who owns property faces property risks simple because such possessions can be destroyed or stolen. Property risks embrace two distinct types of loss: direct loss and indirect or "consequential" loss. Direct loss is the simplest to understand: If a house is destroyed by fire, the owner loses the value of the house. This is a direct loss. However, in addition to losing the value of the building itself, the property owner no longer has a place to live, and during the time required to rebuild the house, it is likely that the owner will incur additional expenses living somewhere else. This loss of use of the destroyed asset is an indirect, or "consequential," loss. An even better example is the case of a business firm. When a firm's facilities are destroyed, it loses not only the value of those facilities but also the income that would have been earned through their use. Property risks, then, can involve two types of losses: (a) the loss of the property and (b) loss of use of the property resulting in lost income or additional expenses.

vii) Liability risks

The basic peril in the liability risk is the unintentional injury of other persons or damage to their property through negligence or carelessness; however, liability may also result from intentional injuries or damage. Under our legal system, the laws provide that one who has injured another, or damaged another's property through negligence or otherwise, can be held responsible for the harm caused. Liability risks therefore involve the possibility of loss of present assets or future income as a result of damages assessed or legal liability arising out of either intentional or unintentional torts, or invasion of the rights of others.

viii) Exchange Rate Risk

This is particularly important for investors that have a large amount of over-seas investment and wish to sell and convert their profit to their home currency. If exchange rate risk is high - even though a substantial profit may have been made overseas, the value of the home currency may be less than the overseas currency and may erode a significant amount of the investments earnings. That is, the more volatile and exchange rate between the home and investment currency, the greater the risk of differing currency value eroding the investments value.

ix) Business Risk

The uncertainty of income caused by the nature of a company's business measured by a ratio of operating earnings. This means that the less certain you are about the income flows of a firm, the less certain the income will flow back to you as an investor. The sources of business risk mainly arises from a company's products/services, ownership support, industry environment, market position, management quality etc. An example of business risk could include a rubbish company that typically would experience stable income and growth over time and would have a low business risk compared to a steel company whereby sales and earnings fluctuate according to need for steel products and typically would have a higher business risk.

xi) Liquidity Risk

The uncertainty introduced by the secondary market for a company to meet its future short term financial obligations. When an investor purchases a security, they expect that at some future period they will be able to sell this security at a profit and redeem this value as cash for consumption this is the liquidity of an investment, its ability to be redeemable for cash at a future date. Generally, as we move up the asset allocation table of the liquidity risk of an investment increases. Liquidity risk arises from situations in which a party interested in trading an asset cannot do it because nobody in the market wants to trade that asset. Liquidity risk becomes particularly important to parties who are about to hold or currently hold an asset, since it affects their ability to trade.

xi) Country Risk

This is also termed political risk, because it is the risk of investing funds in another country whereby a major change in the political or economic environment could occur. This could devalue your investment and reduce its overall return. This type of risk is usually restricted to emerging or developing countries that do not have stable economic or political arenas.

xii) Market Risk: The price fluctuations or volatility increases and decreases in the daily market. This type of risk mainly applies to both stocks and options and tends to perform well in a bull (increasing) market and poorly in a bear (decreasing) market. Generally with stock market risks, the more volatility within the market, the more probability there is that your investment will increase or decrease.

2.12 METHODS OF HANDLING RISKS

Because risk is the possibility of a loss, people, organizations, and society usually try to avoid risk, or, if not avoidable, then to manage it somehow. There are 5 major methods of handling risk:

1. Avoidance
2. Loss control
3. Retention
4. Noninsurance transfers
5. Insurance

1. Avoidance

Avoidance is the elimination of risk. You can avoid the risk of a loss in the stock market by not buying or shorting stocks; the risk of a venereal disease can be avoided by not having sex, or the risk of divorce, by not marrying; the risk of having car trouble, by not having a car. Many manufacturers avoid legal risk by not manufacturing particular products.

Of course, not all risks can be avoided. Notable in this category is the risk of death. But even where it can be avoided, it is often not desirable. By avoiding risk, you may be avoiding many pleasures of life, or the potential profits that result from taking risks. Those who minimize risks by avoiding activities are usually bored with their life and don't make much money. Virtually any activity involves some risk. Where avoidance is not possible or desirable, loss control is the next best thing.

2. Loss control

Loss control can either be affected through loss prevention, which is reducing the probability of risk, or loss reduction, which minimizes the loss. Loss prevention requires identifying the factors that increase the likelihood of a loss, then either eliminating the factors or minimizing their effect. For instance, speeding and driving drunk greatly increase auto accidents. Not driving after drinking alcohol is a method of loss prevention that reduces the probability of an accident. Driving slower is an example of both loss prevention and loss reduction, since it both reduces the probability of an accident and, if an accident does occur, it reduces the magnitude of the losses, since accidents at slower speeds generally cause less damage. Most businesses actively control losses because it is a cost-effective way to prevent losses from accidents and damage to property, and generally becomes more effective the longer the business has been operating, since it can learn from its mistakes.

3. Retention

Risk retention, (aka active retention, risk assumption), is handling the unavoidable or unavoided risk internally, either because insurance cannot be purchased or it is too expensive for the risk, or because it is much more cost-effective to handle the risk internally. Usually, retained risks occur with greater frequency, but have a lower severity. An insurance deductible is a common example of risk retention to save money, since a deductible is a limited risk that can save money on insurance premiums for larger risks.

Businesses actively retain many risks what is commonly called self-insurance because of the cost or unavailability of commercial insurance.

Passive risk retention is retaining risk because the risk is unknown or because the risk taker either does not know the risk or considers it a lesser risk than it actually is. For instance, smoking cigarettes can be considered a form of passive risk retention, since many people smoke without knowing the many risks of disease, and, of the risks they do know, they don't think it will happen to them. Another example is speeding. Many people think they can handle speed, and that, therefore, there is no risk. However, there is always greater risk to speeding, since it always takes longer to stop or change direction, and, in a collision, higher speeds will always result in more damage or risk of serious injury or death, because higher speeds have greater kinetic energy that will be transferred in a collision as damage or injury. Since no driver can possibly foresee every possible event, there will be events that will happen that will be much easier to handle at slower speeds than at higher speeds. For instance, if someone fails to stop at an intersection just as you are driving through, then, at slower speeds, there is obviously a greater chance of avoiding a collision, or, if there is a collision, there will be less damage or injury than would result from a higher speed collision. Hence, speeding is a form of passive risk retention.

4. Noninsurance transfers

Risk can also be managed by noninsurance transfers of risk. The 3 major forms of noninsurance risk transfer are by contract, hedging, and, for business risks, by incorporating. A common way to transfer risk by contract is by purchasing the warranty extension that many retailers sell for the items that they sell. The warranty itself transfers the risk of manufacturing defects from the buyer to the manufacturer. Transfers of risk through contract is often accomplished or prevented by a hold-harmless clause, which may limit liability for the party to which the clause applies.

Hedging is a method of reducing portfolio risk or some business risks involving future transactions. Thus, the possible decline of a stock price can be hedged by buying a put for the stock. A business can hedge a foreign exchange transaction by purchasing a forward contract that guarantees the exchange rate for a future date. Investors can reduce their liability risk in a business by forming a corporation, an S corporation, or a limited liability company. This prevents the extension of the company's liabilities to its investors.

5. Insurance

Insurance is another major method that most people, businesses, and other organizations can use to transfer pure risks, by paying a premium to an insurance company in exchange for a payment of a possible large loss. By using the law of large numbers, an insurance company can estimate fairly reliably the amount of loss for a given number of customers within a specific time. An insurance company can pay for losses because it pools and invests the premiums of many subscribers to pay the few who will have significant losses. Not every pure risk is insurable by private insurance companies. Events which are unpredictable and that could cause extensive damage, such as earthquakes, are not insured by private insurers, although reinsurers may cover these types of risks by relying on statistical models to estimate the probabilities of disaster. Speculative risks are taken in the hope of making a profit are also not insurable, since these risks are taken voluntarily, and, hence, are not pure risks.

2.13 DESCRIBE THE CONCEPT OF RISK MANAGEMENT

Risk management is the identification, assessment, and prioritization of risks followed by coordinated and economical application of resources to minimize, monitor, and control the probability and/or impact of unfortunate events or to maximize the realization of opportunities. Risks can come from uncertainty in financial markets, project failures, legal liabilities, credit risk, accidents, natural causes and disasters as well as deliberate attack from an adversary or events of uncertain root-cause.

The Risk Management is required for any organization to review their risk management strategies and to choose for risk transfer measures like availing insurance cover etc. Many a times the coordination between the technical or operational departments and finance department is difficult and an unbiased study on technical risk management measures adopted and insurance practices followed will help the management of the organization to manage the risk effectively and profitably.

It is very important for insurance industry. Insurance means that insurance companies take over risks from customers. Insurers consider every available quantifiable factor to develop profiles of high and low insurance risk. Level of risk determines insurance premiums. Generally, insurance policies involving factors with greater risk of claims are charged at a higher rate. With much information at hand, insurers can evaluate risk of insurance policies at much higher accuracy.

Some risk managers define risk as the possibility that a future occurrence may cause harm or losses, while noting that risk also may provide possible opportunities. By taking risks, companies sometimes can achieve considerable gains. However, companies need risk management to analyze possible risks in order to balance potential gains against potential losses and avoid expensive mistakes. Risk management is best used as a preventive measure rather than as a reactive measure. Companies benefit most from considering their risks when they are performing well and when markets are growing in order to sustain growth and profitability.

The task of the risk manager is to predict, and enact measures to control or prevent, losses within a company. The risk-management process involves identifying exposures to potential losses, measuring these exposures, and deciding how to protect the company from harm given the nature of the risks and the company's goals and resources. While companies face a host of different risks, some are more important than others. Risk managers determine their importance and ability to be affected while identifying and measuring exposures. For example, the risk of flooding in Arizona would have low priority relative to other risks a company located there might face. Risk managers consider different methods for controlling or preventing risks and then select the best method given the company's goals and resources. After the method is selected and implemented, the method must be monitored to ensure that it produces the intended results.

Meaning of Risk Management

Risk management is a systematic process of identifying and assessing company risks and taking actions to protect a company against them.

2.14 THE EVOLUTION OF RISK MANAGEMENT

The field of risk management emerged in the mid-1970s, evolving from the older field of insurance management. The term risk management was adopted because the new field has a much wider focus than simply insurance management. Risk management includes activities and responsibilities out-side of the general insurance domain, although insurance is an important part of it and insurance agents often serve as risk managers. Insurance management focused on protecting companies from natural disasters and basic kinds of exposures, such as fire, theft, and employee injuries, whereas risk management focuses on these kinds of risks as well as other kinds of costly losses, including those stemming from product liability, employment practices, environmental degradation, accounting compliance, offshore outsourcing, currency fluctuations, and electronic commerce. In the 1980s and 1990s, risk management grew into vital part of company planning and strategy and risk management became integrated with more and more company functions as the field evolved. As the role of risk management has increased to encompass large-scale, organization-wide programs, the field has become known as enterprise risk management.[17]

Environmental risks constitute a significant and growing area of risk management, since reports indicate the number and intensity of natural disasters are increasing. For example, the periodical Risk Management reported that there were about five times as many natural disasters in the 1990s as in the 1960s. The year 2004 was one of the worst in history, with three major hurricanes hitting the state of Florida and a tsunami causing death and devastation in the Pacific Rim. Some observers blame the rising number of natural disasters on global warming, which they believe will cause greater floods, droughts, and storms in the future. Furthermore, any given risk can lead to a variety of losses in different areas. For example, if a fire occurs, a company could lose its physical property such as buildings, equipment, and materials. In this situation, a company also could lose revenues, in that it could no longer produce goods or provide services.

---

[17]Gallant, A. R. (2008). "Stock Prices and Volume", Review of Financial Studies, 5 (2), pp-199–242.

One way managers can assess the risks of doing business is by using the risk calculator developed by Robert Simons, a professor at the Harvard Business School. Although the risk calculator is not a precise tool, it does indicate areas where risks and potential losses exist, such as the rate of expansion and the level of internal competition. Using the risk calculator, managers can determine if their company has a safe or dangerous amount of risk. The risk calculator measures three kinds of internal pressures: risk stemming from growth, corporate culture, and information management. Rapid growth, for example, could be a risk and lead to losses, because if a company grows too quickly, it may not have enough time to train new employees adequately. Hence, unchecked growth could lead to lost sales and diminished quality.

Managers can assess the increased risk associated with growth by determining if sales goals are set by top management without input from employees. If a company sets sales goals in this manner, then it has a high level of risk in that the goals may be too difficult for employees to meet. In cases where employees feel extreme pressure in trying to achieve goals, they may take unnecessary risks. Similarly, companies that rely heavily on performance-based pay also tend to have higher levels of risk.

To assess risk arising from corporate culture, managers should determine what percentage of sales comes from new products or services developed by risk-taking employees. If the percentage is high, then the amount of risk is also high, because such a company depends significantly on new products and the related risks. In addition, a corporate culture that allows or encourages employees to work independently to develop new products increases company risk, as does a high rate of new product or service failures.

Finally, managers can determine business risks resulting from information management by determining if they and their subordinates spend a lot of time gathering information that should already be available. Another way of assessing these risks is by managers considering whether they look at performance data frequently and whether they notice if reports are missing or late.

Risk managers rely on a variety of methods to help companies avoid and mitigate risks in an effort to position them for gains. The four primary methods include exposure or risk avoidance, loss prevention, loss reduction, and risk financing. A simple method of risk management is exposure avoidance, which refers to avoiding products, services, or business activities with the potential for losses, such as manufacturing cigarettes. Loss prevention attempts to root out the potential for losses by implementing such things as employee training and safety programs designed to eradicate risks. Loss reduction seeks to minimize the effects of risks through response systems that neutralize the effects of a disaster or mishap.

The final option risk managers have is to finance risks, paying for them either by retaining or transferring their costs. Companies work with risk managers insofar as possible to avoid risk retention. However, if no other method is available to manage a particular risk, a company must be prepared to cover the losses that is, to retain the losses. The deductible of an insurance policy is an example of a retained loss. Companies also may retain losses by creating special funds to cover any losses.

Risk transferring takes place when a company shares its risk with another party, such as an insurance provider, by getting insurance policies that cover various kinds of risk that can be insured. In fact, insurance constitutes the leading method of risk management. Insurance policies usually cover (a) property risks such as fire and natural disasters, (b) liability risks such as employer's liability and workers' compensation, and (c) transportation risks covering air, land, and sea travel as well as transported goods and transportation liability. Managers of large corporations may decide to manage their risks by acquiring an insurance company to cover part or all of their risks, as many have done. Such insurance companies are called captive insurers.

During the implementation phase, company managers work with risk managers to determine the company goals and the best methods for risk management. Generally, companies implement a combination of methods to control and prevent risks effectively, since these methods are not mutually exclusive, but complementary. After risk management methods have been implemented, risk managers must examine the risk management program to ensure that it continues to be adequate and effective.

2.15 EMERGING AREAS OF RISK MANAGEMENT

In the 1990s, new areas of risk management began to emerge that provide managers with more options to protect their companies against new kinds of exposures. According to the Risk and Insurance Management Society (RIMS), the main trade organization for the risk management profession, among the emerging areas for risk management were operations management, environmental risks, and ethics. As forecast by RIMS, risk managers of corporations started focusing more on verifying their companies' compliance with federal environmental regulations in the 1990s. According to Risk Management, risk managers began to assess environmental risk such as those arising from pollution, waste management, and environmental liability to help make their companies more profitable and competitive. Furthermore, tighter environmental regulations also goaded businesses to have risk managers check their compliance with environmental policies to prevent possible penalties for noncompliance.[18]

Companies also have the option of obtaining new kinds of insurance policies to control risks, which managers and risk managers can take into consideration when determining the best methods for covering potential risks. These non-traditional insurance policies provide coverage of financial risks associated with corporate profits and currency fluctuation. Hence, these policies in effect guarantee a minimum level of profits, even when a company experiences unforeseen losses from circumstances it cannot control. Moreover these non-traditional policies ensure profits for companies doing business in international markets, and hence they help prevent losses from fluctuations in a currency's value. Risk managers can also help alleviate losses resulting from mergers. Stemming from the wave of mergers in the 1990s, risk managers became a more integral part of company merger and acquisition teams.

---

[18]Jennings, R. H., (2009). "Information Dissemination and Portfolio Choice." Journal of Financial and Quantitative Analysis, 18 (3), pp-5–21.

On the buying side, risk managers examine a selling company's expenditures, loss history, insurance policies, and other areas that indicate a company's potential risks. Risk managers also suggest methods for preventing or controlling the risks they find.

Finally, risk managers have been called upon to help businesses manage the risks associated with increased reliance on the Internet. The importance of online business activities in maintaining relationships with customers and suppliers, communicating with employees, and advertising products and services has offered companies many advantages, but also exposed them to new security risks and liability issues. Business managers need to be aware of the various risks involved in electronic communication and commerce and include Internet security among their risk management activities.

2.16 RISK MANAGEMENT OBJECTIVES

A primary objective of risk management is to identify and to manage individual and management risk. Other important objectives are:

i) To concentrate on initial investment and underwriting: Investment decisions are supported by appropriately documented research and analysis and made in accordance with company and client guidelines and objectives. Appropriate recommendations and approvals are obtained to authorize investment decisions.

ii) To focus on Credit Monitoring: Investment agreement terms and covenants are monitored for adherence and reported on an ongoing basis. Changes to investment terms, if any, are approved in accordance with documented limits. Credit risk and investment quality is timely monitored, appropriately categorized, and rated. Periodic reviews, including collateral security reviews, are performed timely, appropriately documented, and results are reported. Remedial action or restructuring plans for loans identified as Especially Mentioned or Watch List are appropriate, timely developed, authorized, and reported to the Quarterly Loan Review Committee.

iii) To manage the investment Portfolio Monitoring: Investment positions and transactions are monitored against company policies and limits and client investment guidelines and objectives. Exceptions of noncompliance are properly reported, escalated to senior management, and the resolution is properly authorized. Third-party investments acquired are allocated to investment accounts on a reasonable and fair basis.

iv) To ensure trading transactions: Trading transactions for publics are accurate, complete, and properly authorized.

v) Valuation and Pricing: Publics — Portfolios are accurately valued using independent sources on a timely basis and reported to senior management. Discrepancies are researched and resolved timely. Privates — Valuation of private investments is appropriate and documented.

vi) Performance Monitoring: Performance measurement, ranking, and attribution analysis is regularly performed, reviewed, reported, and approved.

vii) Policies, Procedures, Authorities, and Responsibilities: Policies, procedures, authorities, and responsibilities are clearly defined and communicated. Employees have the necessary knowledge, information, and tools to manage relevant risks and support the achievement of the business unit's objectives.

viii) Management Information: Management information is sufficient and timely. Performance is monitored against targets and indicators. Follow-up procedures are established and performed.

2.17 RISK MANAGEMENT PROCESS

Risk analysis is best done in a group with each member of the group having a good understanding of the tasks and objectives of the area being analyzed. The various steps of risk management process are:

Step-1: Identify the Risks

As a group, list the things that might inhibit your ability to meet your objectives. You can even look at the things that would actually enhance your ability to meet those objectives e.g. a fund-raising commercial opportunity. These are the risks that you face eg. loss of a key team member; prolonged IT network outage; delayed provision of important information by another work unit/individual; failure to seize a commercial opportunity etc.

Step-2: Identify the Causes

Try to identify what might cause these things to occur eg. the key team member might be disillusioned with his/her position, might be head hunted to go elsewhere; the person upon whom you are relying for information might be very busy, going on leave or notoriously slow in supplying such data; the supervisor required to approve the commercial undertaking might be risk averse and need extra convincing before taking the risk etc.

Step-3: Identify the Controls

Identify all the things (Controls) that you have in place that are aimed at reducing the Likelihood of your risks from happening in the first place and, if they do happen, what you have in place to reduce their impact (Consequence) e.g. providing a friendly work environment for your team; multi-skill across the team to reduce the reliance on one person; stress the need for the required information to be supplied in a timely manner; send a reminder before the deadline; provide additional information to the supervisor before he/she asks for it etc.

Step-4: Establish your Likelihood and Consequence

Descriptors, remembering that these depend upon the context of your analysis i.e. if your analysis relates to your work unit, any financial loss or loss of a key staff member, for example, will have a greater impact on that work unit than it will have on the University as a whole so those descriptors used for the whole-of-University (strategic) context will generally not be appropriate for the Faculty, other work unit or the individual e.g., a loss of $300000 might be considered Insignificant to the University, but it could very well be Catastrophic to your work unit.

Step-5: Establish your Risk Rating Descriptors

Risk Rating Descriptors i.e., what is meant by a Low, Moderate, High or Extreme Risk needs to be decided upon ahead of time. Because these are more generic in terminology though, you might find that the University's Strategic Risk Rating Descriptors are applicable.

Step-6: Add other Controls

Generally speaking, any risk that is rated as High or Extreme should have additional controls applied to it in order to reduce it to an acceptable level. What the appropriate additional controls might be, whether they can be afforded, what priority might be placed on them etc. is something for the group to determine in consultation with the Head of the work unit who, ideally, should be a member of the group doing the analysis in the first place.

Step-7: Make a Decision

Once the above process is complete, if there are still some risks that are rated as High or Extreme, a decision has to be made as to whether the activity will go ahead. There will be occasions when the risks are higher than preferred but there may be nothing more that can be done to mitigate that risk i.e. they are out of the control of the work unit but the activity must still be carried out. In such situations, monitoring the circumstances and regular review is essential.

Step-8: Monitor and Review

The monitoring of all risks and regular review of the unit's risk profile is an essential element for a successful risk management program.

2.18 IMPORTANCE OF RISK MANAGEMENT

Importance of Risk Management can be summarized as follows:

1. It is easier to spot projects in trouble

Risk management practices let you see where projects need attention, and which projects these are. Dovetailing perfectly with any existing Project Management Office processes you already have in place, good risk management can give you the context for understanding the performance of a project and contribute to any health checks, peer reviews or audits.

2. There are fewer surprises

Leaders typically don't like surprises! A robust approach to managing risk allows teams to better communicate about project challenges in a more timely way. Risk management practices let the team spot concerns far earlier. Early awareness of potential problems means that the right people can intervene to mitigate a problem before it becomes too severe to do anything about. It also avoids the 'project manager as hero' scenario, and lots of firefighting, which is generally an expensive and high-effort way to fix problems. Managing risks are before they materialize makes for fewer sensational headlines but a smoother, more efficient and cost-effective way of running your business.

3. There's better quality data for decision making

Senior leaders have access to better quality and more helpful data which enables them to make better decisions more grounded in the reality of a project. Being able to access risk information in real time through a project management dashboard means that decisions are made based on the latest data, not a report that is already out of date before it reaches the Exec team.

4. Communication is elevated

Good risk management elevates the conversation. It creates a point of discussion between project teams and key senior stakeholders, prompting them to discuss the difficult topics and deal with potential causes of conflict. Suppliers are involved in the conversations too, as risk responses necessarily touch on their activities. Including them in risk management discussions can create more positive working relationships with their key personnel, because they'll see that their success is tied to the success of the project and that there is willingness to work as a whole team to do something about it. The conversation can be framed in what is good for the project and the enterprise, instead of either being too caught up in the detail or affected by internal politics. An increase in dialogue, and the content of that dialogue, brings the team closer together as a working group.

5. Budgets rely less on guesswork

Project risk management means that contingency budgets can be more accurately estimated and rely less on the professional guesstimates of the project team. By incorporating risk management into schedule planning and cost planning you can create scenarios to better inform what you should be budgeting in terms of extra time, resource and money.

6. The expectation of success is set

Knowing that risk is being actively managed sets an expectation for project success. With the framework in place to deliver despite the known risks, and open communication about the project's challenges with senior managers, everyone begins work knowing that success is the expected outcome. This changes the whole mindset of the team: knowing they are working on something destined to deliver great results for the company improves morale, supports productivity and hopefully engenders and environment where success is achieved.

7. The team remains focused

With risks being actively tracked and managed, the project team can maintain a focus on the critical outcomes. Risk management supports this because it serves to highlight where project outcomes may not be achieved, focusing the team on what to do about that particular concern to get the project back on track. With risk management shining a light on the areas of challenge within a project, the team can move swiftly to deal with them, ensuring that actions are taken to mitigate the risk and deliver successfully. This prevents problems from being overlooked in the busyness of the day-to-day work on a project – especially when those problems appear to be difficult to solve.

8. Escalations are clearer and easier

When a project team can't deal with a risk themselves, they need to escalate it to senior management for advice and action. Clear risk management processes take the guesswork out of when this should happen. A defined process ensures that important risks are seen and assessed by the right people at the right time, enabling early action as required to better address a potential problem.

2.19 ADVANTAGES OF RISK MANAGEMENT PROCESS

Risk management process is considered as an important discipline that the business has in its recent times. Many organizations tend to realize the advantages of enterprise risk management. Following are few benefits of risk management in projects:

a. Benefits of risk identification

Risk identification helps in fostering the vigilance in times of discipline and calm at the times of crisis. It implies all the risks in prior that are most likely to happen and are planned to execute without any assumptions that run. These positive risks are often held upon most of the occurrences. It helps in opportunity risks so as to be aware of the forthcoming issues.

b. Benefits of risk assessment

It focuses on the identified tasks on assisting the impact of business or projects. This phase focuses on the ideas that are discussed among the stakeholders. It has greatest advantage of dealing with the points that are finalized with more possible solutions. It has sense of all views that turns into accountability of each and every social life. Participation in these kinds of assessments will help one to tackle his/her risks. It promotes organizational culture.

c. Treatment of risks

It helps in treating one's own risks that are the subsets of implementing a plan. It has internal compliance that are brought and mitigated towards the forsaken actions. Its opportunity falls in the lack of preparation and even more realized upon the profitable data that relieves through internal controls.

d. Minimization of risks

The risks that are handled within the given assessments plans are foreseen within the business functions. It enables one to speed up the data to change policies and contingencies that are made successful within the mapped business functions. Here the cost beneficial analysis is to be revised within the ownership of risks. It focuses on change of policies within the detailed structural behavior.

e. Awareness about the risks

Here the terms that are noticed will create awareness among the scheduled terms of risks that are a successful analysis and evaluation of exercising the modules of risks. It enables one to concentrate on the risk treatments within the lessons learnt and are scheduled into lack of preparation. It has subsequent phases regarding each module within the identified data.

f. Successful business strategies

Risk management strategy is not one-time activity and the grade points are finalized within the recent status. It has different stages that modulate to lack of preparation, planning and successful implementations of all the plans. It has operational efficiency that is realized upon the mitigation of negative risks. It has contingent policies over the preparation of business in the measures of treatment.

g. Saving cost and time

It threats to the task that is completed over the projects and the other business strategies. It always results in saving the costs that are consolidated within the items that are practiced. It prevents wastage and make up the time for firefighting.

h. New opportunities

The opportunities that are emerging are held within the new ways of communicating on the unravel issues. It has collective and least significant part that matches with most of the scenarios. It prepares for the future endeavors and the related exhaustive efforts as inputs.

i. Harvesting knowledge

Here one must try to spend the knowledge about the stakeholder's experience of the preemptive approach that are made applicable for the unprepared threats towards the knowledge gained and this provides a template to face the readymade risks. It has successive plans that are indulged from the start till the collective knowledge.

j. Protecting resources

The risk management plans and policies under help in protecting the resources of the organization. This helps in promoting the resources instead of using them illegally. It also equips safety among the adaptive changes to the staff alternatives and is bundled together with the other resources. It builds production plans and the alternative plans or the process of re-routing.

k. Improvement in credit ratings

The improvement in credit ratings evolves numerous agencies that support the accomplished tasks resulting in lower budget investments. It has capital volatility that translates the greater confidence issues particularly with the stakeholders. It aims at building multiple business aspects that have tangible benefits.

l. Regulatory compliances

This framework helps in meeting regulatory needs. It performs and measures the risk managements. This improvement helps in attaining the higher credit aspects. It also derives higher efficiency towards the capital volatility and even the rating metrics that are assigned to the compensated business plans. It translates into greater confidence of improved stakeholders that are made applicable within the insured business.

m. Values shareholders

It aims at the borrowing capacity of the shareholder that has significant effort within the management and assumes the determinant roles that the company can extend to. It has exact decision making process within the current models and also the expected regulatory recruitment.

n. Possibilities of risks

It dictates the clear possibilities of risk that are managed within the severity or impact of the organization that are updated to own risk strategies. It has insight of real balance sheets that supports the culture of risk management. It modulates the designed data and even the approach towards the compatible and the insight of balancing. It supports all the ordinary requirements of a plan.

o. Faster competition

When the organization contributes to different levels of budgets with the people of various skills set, the commitment towards the work will be more. It achieves competitive advantage on the logic schedules that are better. It has the deepest level of managing risks. These competitions are managed within the up and downs of entire life.

p. Provides support

It provides support to the organization that is handled between both the chances of achieving and losing the financial plans. Here the benefits of financial risk management are uninformed at both the level of improving chances to make the acquisition of achieving potential breakthrough in the supply chain. It has concentrated support of the chances of achieving the pre-planned financial activities.

q. Identification of risks

Risk management system helps in identifying the risks that have precise network to determine the optimal management of risks. It has the maximized opportunity of the risks that are relevant in implementing the guidance provided. It has holistic support from the entire organization when the risks are identified. It will become streamlined and efficient within the complex elements.

r. Provides guidance

It provides prior guidance about the framework that are enabled within the experience and assessing the risks that are modeled within the strategies of risk. It has development of advanced risk management techniques that are interrelated within the consequences of the gained knowledge and the other risks.

s. Identification of possible threats

This identification provides compensatory mundane activities that aim at motivating the employees to gather information about the consequent changes. It spends time on the research and development of the execution of maintenance strategies. It accustoms the employees within the persuaded timing.

t. Reduces impact and loss

Risk management has more defined proceedings when there is pre-planned schedule or loss of the object. It contributes a part to stress and worry. The complexity matters when they are gathered. Here it ensures the organization with all possible outcomes of the independent and objective assessments that are analyzed on taking challenges.

q. Stability of earnings

The business operations that are held within the next operation level will concentrate more on the scheduled amount of data. It reduces the impact of business activities. Employees will be retrenched so as to keep in the comfort zone.

r. Managing the strategic plans

Managing risks has the strategic plans that are related to the plans that are most used in various strategic plans. This manages the data that depends on the most of the resources that are linked to the migration defined data. It reflects on the generated data that manages most of the generated cash flows that are in adverse situations.

s. Handling previous projects

If the analyzing of risk is done correctly in the previous stages, then it can be moved without processing the detailed information along various channels of risks. This memory can be held to unfold the future risks that are conflicted within the schematic schedule. It enlarges new risk towards the competitors that are managed within the forbidden strategies.

t. Nurturing risks

Each possibility of the risks will be accompanied by the different logics that can compensate within the rigid comparisons and the choices made defining the aligned decision makers of each project. This requires well trained operators so as to optimize the situations of risks.

u. Collaborated work

Risks focuses payoff and even to yield the profit. Sometimes the mistakes done can also be productive. It manages the possibility to perform the tasks with the organizational behavior. Here managers are encouraged to focus on the risks that can be defined as exploitable challenging proposals.

2.20 DISADVANTAGES OF RISK MANAGEMENT PROCESS

Managing the risks provides the waste of time to compensate the projects. It persuades the projects that reciprocate to improve the funds in the company. It is spent on the research and development of the allocated issues that hold to ensure project management.

a. Complex calculations

Risk management involves complex calculations in terms of managing risks. Without the automatic tool, each and every calculation regarding risks becomes difficult. It involves the ideal data that contributes to the employee's standards. This process is really difficult to predict.

b. Unmanaged losses

If the organization meddles with a loss, then that pay will be delivered to the pay loss of the firm. Here, the organization is responsible for the loss that happened due to improper schedule about the risk management.

c. Ambiguity

Even if the ambiguity is out of loss then people have to cover it within the planned scale of losses of the discounts and even the consideration into unnecessary insurance discounts.

d. Depends on external entities

Managing risks depends on the external entities that are modulated within the organization, usually depends on the external data. It includes all the dependent information about the risks regarding other valid resources. The transferable resources depend on the external entities that tend to have data.

e. Mitigation

Usually, mitigation guarantees losses of the concealed impairment of money which may cause improper management of risks. This leads to unsafe acceptance of data within rare company losses.

f. Difficulty in implementing

Risk management takes a long time to gather the information regarding the strategic plans. It has universal standards that are mitigated and accepted according to the monetary values. It matches with the hard understanding without recent experience without compensation of the required quantity of data.

g. Performance

Since the risk management can be processed only with subjectivity, it holds on the control of prospects within each issue. It can be identified with the difficult implementation of controls. It manages the cost benefits analysis that is not implemented. This process concentrates more on the implementation of controls.

h. Potential threats

These potential threats are to be maintained carefully so as to organize and disappear from the market. This implementation reduces the level of risk and proportionally increases the control over it. Any kind of process will have its own limitations and benefits of project risk management. Thus to build an effective risk management one has to focus on the mitigated strategic plans of risks that are effective on the risk takers. It is to identify the maximum of the entire management to overcome forthcoming dangers.

Risk management becomes the major case when the organization has targeted results apart from the potential threats, damages and vulnerabilities.

2.21 NATURE OF THE STUDY

The research study was Empirical in nature and the required data were collected through experimentation or observation of the researcher. This was needed to observe the respondents (i.e., Stock market expert, Investors of Gold Futures, Gold Sellers and Stock Brokers) and their reactions towards Dimensions of Gold Futures with special reference to Bullion Market. The researcher noted down all matters as a source of information during semi-structured interview, discussion and data collection through questionnaire. The stock market brokers were the sources of real time bullion market information to compare the fluctuation of market rates, risk factors, investment opportunities with respects to several countries point of view.

The main purpose of the research work was to identify the dimensions of gold futures with reference to bullion markets. The investors of gold futures were another source or reason for information collection.

Hence to conclude, this chapter covers the nature and areas of hedging, classification of hedging , hedging strategies, gold hedge performance , advantages and disadvantages of hedging. The concept of risk and its management, various risks in bullion market and methods of handling such risks, emerging areas of risk management, objectives process and importance along with the advantage and disadvantages of risk management process is being covered under this chapter.

CHAPTER - 3
REVIEW OF LITERATURE

The concept of Dimensions of Gold Futures with special reference to Bullion Market is by no means new and the number of research studies published in this area is still growing, so carving out original research is not so easier. This study focuses on the rapidly growing segment of Dimensions of Gold Futures with special reference to Bullion Market. Exploration of the various Journal Articles with the term "Bullion", "Bullion Market", "Gold Futures", "Hedging", "Risk" and "Risk Management" in their titles, keywords and abstracts yields more than 130 peer-reviewed and non-peer reviewed articles were appeared. During the time 2013 to 2016, more than 170 Books were reviewed with the term "The Bombay Bullion Market", "Bullion and Foreign Exchanges", "Indian Bullion Market", "Bombay Stock Exchange" etc. as keywords.

There is plenty of literature available on the topic of derivative instruments. Many text books and the relevant websites provide good coverage on the subject. The purpose of literature review is innumerable in research work. Specific need for references and citations makes secondary data quite valid. Literature review forms the integral part of larger research. Secondary data forms the sole basis for research. Literature reviews provides support to validate secondary data .Hence complementing the field data conclusion. It has also been observed that secondary data gives insight into the research details. It is mandatory to examine secondary data as a prerequisite for accuracy and relevance for primary data and subsequent analysis. Literature review heavily relied on published texts, technical reports, fundamental analysis of stock futures and index futures, other manuals, internet, journals and case studies in the field of hedging were constantly reviewed.

Mohan Nandhaa and Shawkat Hammoudeh (2007). described in the article "Systematic risk, and oil price and exchange rate sensitivities in Asia-Pacific stock markets", that the relationship between beta risk and realized stock index return in the presence of oil and exchange rate sensitivities for 15 countries in the Asia-Pacific region using the international factor model. Thirteen of the 15 countries have the expected beta signs and show significant sensitivity to domestic risk when the world stock market is in both up and down modes. In terms of oil sensitivity, only the Philippines and South Korea are oil-sensitive to changes in the oil price in the short run, when the price is expressed in local currency only. Basically no country shows sensitivity to oil price measured in US dollar regardless whether the oil market is up or down. Nine countries are affected by changes in the exchange rate.

Andrew C. Worthington (2007), explained in the article "Gold investment as an inflationary hedge: co-integration evidence with allowance for endogenous structural breaks", that the note tests for the presence of a stable long-run relationship between the price of gold and inflation in the United States from 1945 to 2006 and from 1973 to 2006. Since both the gold market and the inflationary regime have been subjected to structural change over time, a novel unit root testing procedure is employed which allows for the timing of significant breaks to be estimated, rather than assumed exogenous. After taking these breaks into account, a modified co-integration approach provides strong evidence of a co-integrating relationship between gold and inflation in the post-war period and since the early 1970s. The results lend support to the widely held view that direct and indirect gold investment can serve as an effective inflationary hedge.

John Betts and Kunal Mamik (2008) in the article "Optimal Hedging Decisions for Gold Miners: How Much Future Production Should a Gold Miner Forward Sell?" attempts to answer the question of how much of its current production a gold producer should hedge by forward selling. We develop a model which allows a company manager to determine the optimal hedge, and an estimate of the risk of company failure, based on an estimate of the forward price of gold; the mine's operating costs; and the company's tolerance to debt. The model is illustrated with data drawn from historical gold prices and recent Australian company data. By simulating multiple instances of companies operating with different degrees of forward selling under varying levels of volatility in the price of gold, it was shown that the optimal degree of forward selling increased as volatility increased. The model allows managers to gain insights into the effect of volatility on a company's return given its particular cost structure which in turn, supports more informed decision making.

G. William Schwert (2008). Explained in the article "Why Does Stock Market Volatility Change Over Time?" that the relation of stock volatility with real and nominal macroeconomic volatility, economic activity, financial leverage and stock trading activity using monthly data from 1857 to 1987. An important fact, previously noted by Officer, is that stock return variability was unusually high during the 1929–1939 Great Depression. While aggregate leverage is significantly correlated with volatility, it explains a relatively small part of the movements in stock volatility. The amplitude of the fluctuations in aggregate stock volatility is difficult to explain using simple models of stock valuation, especially during the Great Depression.

Mark P. Taylor and Helen Allen (2008), defined in the article "The use of technical analysis in the foreign exchange market" that the analysis of financial markets involves providing forecasts or trading advice on the basis of largely visual inspection of past prices, without regard to any underlying economic or 'fundamental' analysis. This paper reports the results of a questionnaire survey, conducted on behalf of the Bank of England, among chief foreign exchange dealers based in London in November 1988. Amongst other findings, it is revealed that at least 90 per cent of respondents place some weight on this form of non-fundamental analysis when forming views at one or more time horizons. There is also a skew towards reliance on technical, as opposed to fundamentalist, analysis at shorter horizons, which becomes steadily reversed as the length of horizon considered is increased. A very high proportion of chief dealers view technical and fundamental analysis as complementary forms of analysis and a substantial proportion suggest that technical advice may be self-fulfilling.

John Childs (2008). Described in the article "Reforming small-scale mining in sub-Saharan Africa: Political and ideological challenges to a Fair Trade gold initiative", that the sub-Saharan Africa, artisanal and small-scale mining (ASM) has caused a range of environmental, social and economic problems. Most of the donor support pledged to improve conditions in the sector to date, however, has failed to facilitate marked improvements, in large part because emphasis has been placed on technical interventions; at the same time, impoverished miners' needs and concerns have been seriously overlooked. It is against this background that this paper critically examines the underpinnings and potential of "Fair Trade gold" as a solution to many of the problems plaguing the ASM sector and a mechanism for alleviating the hardships of its operators. Unlike the majority of ASM-support support measures implemented in the past, "Fair Trade gold" is entrenched in the discourse of "partnership" and "participation". To ensure its effectiveness initiatives must be adapted according to the specificities of ASM.

René M. Stulz (2009). Examine in the article "Rethinking Risk Management", that the theory of corporate risk management that attempts to go beyond the "variance-minimization" model that dominates most academic discussions of the subject. It argues that the primary goal of risk management is not to dampen swings in corporate cash flows or value, but rather to provide protection against the possibility of costly lower-tail outcomes–situations that would cause financial distress or make a company unable to carry out its investment strategy. By eliminating downside risk and reducing the expected costs of financial trouble, risk management can also help a company to achieve both its optimal capital structure and its optimal ownership structure. For, besides increasing corporate debt capacity, the reduction of downside risk also encourages larger equity stakes for managers by shielding their investments from "uncontrollables."

James Dow (2009). Explained in the article "Arbitrage, Hedging, and Financial Innovation", that the costs and benefits of introducing a new security in a standard framework where uninformed traders with hedging needs interact with risk-averse informed traders. Opening a new market may make everybody worse off, even when the new security is traded in equilibrium. This article emphasizes cross-market links between hedging and speculative demands: risk-averse arbitrageurs can use the new market to hedge their positions in the preexisting security, which can affect liquidity in the old market. More generally, the availability of such hedging opportunities will influence the strategies to which traders will direct resources.

Lisa Meulbroek (2009). Defined in the article "A Comparison of Forward and Futures Prices of an Interest Rate-Sensitive Financial Asset" that the paper focuses on contractual distinctions as an explanation for the price divergence between futures and forward contracts. Specifically, it investigates the effect of marking-to-market on the observed price differences using the pricing model described. Using previously unavailable data, this paper employs Eurodollars, an interest rate-sensitive financial asset, to test the CIR model. Unlike prior empirical studies, test results support both the weak prediction concerning the sign of the average price difference and the stronger prediction that specific covariances explain the variation in the price differences.

Muneeb Ahmed (2010). Described in the article "Hedging With Gold Futures" that the world market has seen a decline in currency. Some currencies have obviously been affected more than others. This has definitively had a major impact on the price of gold. Specifically, the price of gold per ounce has skyrocketed as a result. Portfolios have experienced hugely positive results. This leads us to our next point: gold futures work as an effective hedge. For those not familiar with the term "hedge", this deals with items in a portfolio designed to offset losses. In other words, the gains in certain items in a portfolio are intended to provide the much-needed boost to what may otherwise be declining values. A portfolio represents an investor's overall net worth. For most investors, the answer would clearly be a yes. That would necessitate the search for an item that can effectively work as a legitimate hedge. With gold futures, there is somewhat less risk since gold has been performing so well in recent years.

P K Mishra and J R Das (2010). Explained in the article "Gold Price Volatility and Stock Market Returns in India", that the capital market of a country in terms of a wide range of macroeconomic and financial variables has been the subject matter of many researches since last few decades. Recently one such variable, that is, gold price volatility has attracted the attention of many researchers, academicians and analysts. Thus, this paper is an attempt to analyse the causality relation that may run between domestic gold prices and stock market returns in India. The study by taking into consideration the domestic gold prices and stock market returns based on BSE 100 index, investigates the Granger causality in the Vector Error Correction Model for the period January 1991 to December 2009. The analysis provides the evidence of feedback causality between the variables. It infers that the Gold prices Granger-causes stock market returns and stock market returns also Granger-causes the gold prices in India during the sample period. Thus, both the variables contain some significant information for the prediction of one in terms of another.

Ian Domowitz and Craig S Hakkio (2010). Analysed in the article "Conditional variance and the risk premium in the foreign exchange market" that the investigate the existence of a risk premium in the foreign exchange market, based on the conditional variance of market forecast errors. The forecast errors are assumed to follow the ARCH process introduced by Engle. Estimation and diagnostic testing of the model are discussed, and results are presented for the currencies of the United Kingdom, France, Germany, Japan and Switzerland. The price of gold peaked in 2011 at $1,921, and has been on a slide ever since. It now trades at south of $1,200 (as of mid-March 2014). Erb and Harvey note in their paper "The Golden Dilemma," that gold has positive price elasticity. That basically means that as more people buy gold the price goes up in line with demand. It also means there isn't any underlying "fundamental" to the price of gold.

Oleksandr Pavlov and Li Yan Jing YANG (2011) examined "Hedging with Gold Futures: Evidence from China and India" that the recently the National Commodity & Derivatives Exchange (NCDEX) and the Shanghai Futures Exchange (SHFE) introduced gold futures trading in India and China respectively. In developing markets like China and India it is important to manage risk. For the sake of choosing the optimal hedge strategy it is sufficient to understand and calculate the optimal hedge ratio. Therefore we divide our analyze on two parts. Firstly, we calculate optimal hedge ratios for hedging spot contracts with futures contracts. Secondly, we evaluate the hedging efficiency of these optimal hedge ratios. It is found that for both China and India VAR-MGARCH model estimates of the time varying hedge ratio give higher volatility reduction compare to the hedge ratios based on models with constant hedge ratio. Overall, gold futures contracts in China and India prove to be a smart and well-needed hedging tool for clever investor.

Philippe Jorion (2011). Described in the article "Predicting Volatility in the Foreign Exchange Market" that the measures of volatility implied in option prices are widely believed to be the best available volatility forecasts. In this article, we examine the information content and predictive power of implied standard deviations (ISDs) derived from Chicago Mercantile Exchange options on foreign currency futures. The article finds that statistical time-series models, even when given the advantage of "ex post" parameter estimates, are outperformed by ISDs. ISDs, however, also appear to be biased volatility forecasts. Using simulations to investigate the robustness of these results, the article finds that measurement errors and statistical problems can substantially distort inferences. Even accounting for these, however, ISDs appear to be too variable relative to future volatility.

Catherine Schrand and Haluk Unal (2012). Describe in the article "Hedging and Coordinated Risk Management: Evidence from Thrift Conversions" that the explanation for hedging as a means of allocating rather than reducing risk. We argue that when increases in total risk are costly, firms optimally allocate risk by reducing (increasing) exposure to risks that provide zero (positive) economic rents. Our evidence shows that mutual thrifts that convert to stock institutions increase total risk following conversion, consistent with their increased abilities and incentives for risk taking. They achieve this increase by hedging interest-rate risk and increasing credit risk. We provide some evidence that risk-management activities are related to growth capacity and management compensation structure attained at conversion.

Saurabh Singh and Swati Saharawat (2012) described in the article 'Hedging dynamics with gold futures' that the people view gold as a reliable source of value in times of difficulty. Gold offers insurance against stock market failure. While at the same amongst the different purposes that require use of Gold, certainly include commodity uses. Other assets are dependent upon a certain government or political climate to retain value or appreciate, but gold is largely independent of political climate. The research design adopted for the completion of the study was of descriptive type. Every investor wants to hedge his/her risk against to the price fluctuations before investing in gold, and the right path for this can be investing in Gold Futures with knowledge of Basis. Taking a deep look at the above reasons and broad subject area of hedging the present study was undertaken to understand the nature and functioning mechanism of Basis used to minimize the risk for gold investors, understand different markets for hedgers and suggest some strategies to them for minimizing their risk. The study leads to the conclusion that by keeping an eye on movement of 'Basis and of market the importers and exporters' can manage the four scenarios for both long/short hedgers.

Masahiro Kawa and Itzhak Zilcha (2012). Defined in the article "International trade with forward-futures markets under exchange rate and price uncertainty" that the examines a risk-averse firm's decisions on the level of trade, when the exchange rate and the commodity price are uncertain, and the extent of forward exchange and commodity futures commitments. First we verify the Separation Theorem and the Full Double Hedging Theorem. Second, we investigate the implications of the existence of both forward foreign exchange and commodity futures markets in comparison to the case where only one (or no) market is available to the firm. The second exercise enables us to focus on conditions under which establishing forward-futures arrangements promotes international trade.

Peter M. DeMarzo and Darrell Duffie (2013). Examine in the article "Corporate Incentives for Hedging and Hedge Accounting" that the information affect of financial risk management. Financial hedging improves the informativeness of corporate earnings as a signal of management ability and project quality by eliminating extraneous noise. Managerial and shareholder incentives regarding information transmission may differ, however, leading to conflicts regarding an optimal hedging policy. We show that these incentives depend on the accounting information made available by the firm. Under some circumstances, if hedge transactions are not disclosed (i.e., firms report only aggregate earnings), managers hedge to achieve greater risk reduction than they would if full disclosure were required. In these cases, it is optimal for shareholders to request only aggregate accounting reports.

Christopher J Clarke and Suvir Varma (2013). Described in the article "Strategic risk management: the new competitive edge" that the Risk Management has become a critical issue as a result of globalization and the continued quest for greater returns. Whilst most companies now see risk as a key strategic issue, risk is typically still treated tactically and piecemeal. In this article, the authors argue that an integrated risk management approach allows companies to consistently deliver superior performance while proactively managing risks. The article outlines a structured methodology for risk management process evaluation and change. The methodology has been developed through the authors' work as risk management consultants to various companies globally.

Joanne Hill and Thomas Schneeweis (2013). Analyse in the article "The Hedging Effectiveness of Foreign Currency Futures" that the study provides an initial analysis of the hedging potential of the foreign currency futures markets. Numerous studies exist on the pricing efficiency and hedging effectiveness of the foreign currency forward markets, but little research exists on the foreign currency futures market. An adequate price history has only recently become available to carry out such an investigation. Minimum risk hedges and hedging effectiveness measures are presented for five currencies: the British pound, German mark, Canadian dollar, Japanese yen and Swiss franc. Analysis indicates the relative desirability of positions in futures contracts to minimize the risk of spot currency exposure. Results also show hedging effectiveness increases with the investment horizon.

Haluk Unal (2013). Examine in the article "Hedging and Risk Management" that the paper departs from standard finance theory in suggesting that some companies may have a comparative advantage in bearing certain financial market risks–an advantage that derives from information acquired through their normal business activities. Although such specialized information may lead some companies to take speculative positions in commodities or currencies, it is more likely to encourage "selective" hedging, a practice in which the risk manager's "view" of future price movements influences the percentage of the exposure that is hedged. But, to the extent that such view-taking becomes an accepted part of a company's risk management program, it is important to evaluate managers' bets on a risk-adjusted basis and relative to the market. If risk managers want to behave like money managers, they should be evaluated like money managers.

Jeffrey M. Christian (2013) defined in the article "Gold bar demand dives in the Chinese Gold Bullion Market" that the economic reforms over the last three decades enabled the Chinese gold market to grow into what it is today. The Chinese government has been deregulating its gold market since the late 1980s, and since 2001 has largely removed itself from gold and silver market trading activities within China. The Chinese market deregulation was designed to unleash growth in domestic gold production and demand. Previously, the buying and selling of gold was largely controlled by China's central bank, the People's Bank of China (PBOC). PBOC no longer requires all gold to be bought and sold through its network. Most of the gold transactions were shifted to a dealer market that already existed but matured with deregulation, and the Shanghai Gold Exchange (SGE), which has played an integral role in facilitating the trading of physical gold among producers, consumers, and investors.

Dirk G. Baur (2013). Explained in the article "Asymmetric Volatility in the Gold Market" that the volatility of equity returns generally exhibits an asymmetric reaction to positive and negative shocks. Economic explanations for this phenomenon are leverage and a volatility feedback effect. This paper studies the volatility of gold and demonstrates that there is an inverted asymmetric reaction to positive and negative shocks, i.e. positive shocks increase the volatility by more than negative shocks. The paper argues that this effect is related to the safe haven property of gold. Investors interpret positive gold price changes as a signal for future adverse conditions and uncertainty in other asset markets. This introduces uncertainty in the gold market and thus higher volatility. The empirical results hold for gold bullion and gold coins denominated in different currencies, for different return frequencies, sample periods and distributional assumptions. Finally, we show that the inverted volatility effect of gold can lower the aggregate risk of a portfolio for specific correlation levels.

Chia-Lin Changa and Jui-Chuan (2013). Explained in the article "Dynamic price integration in the global gold market", that the inter-relationships among gold prices in five global gold markets, namely London, New York, Japan, Hong Kong (since 1 July 1997, a Special Administrative Region (SAR) of China), and Taiwan. We investigate the linkages between Taiwan and the other global gold markets to provide insights for useful investment strategies. The augmenting level-VAR models proposed by Toda and Yamamoto (1995) show that the empirical results find bi-directional causality between the London and New York gold markets, and uni-directional causality from New York to the other markets. In this sense, the New York market has gained a leading role in affecting global gold markets. This empirical finding serves as a predictor for the gold price in global markets.

Edel Tully and Brian M. Lucey (2013). describes in the article "A power GARCH examination of the gold market" that the power term is estimated within the model rather than specified by the authors. This paper examines both cash and futures prices of gold and significant economic variables over the 1983–2003 period, with special focus on two periods, around the 1987 and 2001 equity market crashes. Modestly sized project finance related hedging agreements are also a strong possibility, although a number of recent announcements have highlighted the growing significance of streaming agreements as a component of new finance arrangements. However, in the absence of a large-scale hedge this year so far, it seems increasingly unlikely that substantial net hedging will be the end result for 2015, unless a major new hedge is undertaken. Based on the activity reported to date, we now consider it probable that modest net de-hedging will be the outcome for the year, the report said.

Matthew Hood and Farooq Malik (2013). defined in the article "Is gold the best hedge and a safe haven under changing stock market volatility", that the role of gold and other precious metals relative to volatility (Volatility Index (VIX)) as a hedge (negatively correlated with stocks) and safe haven (negatively correlated with stocks in extreme stock market declines) using data from the US stock market. Using daily data from November 1995 to November 2010, we find that gold, unlike other precious metals, serves as a hedge and a weak safe haven for US stock market. However, we find that VIX serves as a very strong hedge and a strong safe haven during our sample period. We also find that in periods of extremely low or high volatility, gold does not have a negative correlation with the US stock market. We highlight the practical significance of our results for financial market participants by conducting a portfolio analysis.

Scott H. Irwin and Dwight R. Sanders (2013). Disclosed in the article "Index Funds, Financialization, and Commodity Futures Markets, that the market participants and policy-makers believe that index fund investment was a major driver of the 2007-2008 spike in commodity futures prices. One group of empirical studies does find evidence that commodity index investment had an impact on the level of futures prices. However, the data and methods used in these studies are subject to criticisms that limit the confidence one can place in their results. Moreover, another group of studies provides no systematic evidence of a relationship between positions of index funds and the level of commodity futures prices. The lack of a direct empirical link between index fund trading and commodity futures prices casts considerable doubt on the belief that index funds fueled a price bubble.

Viral V. Acharya and Lars A. Lochstoer (2013). Defined in the article "Limits to arbitrage and hedging: Evidence from commodity markets" that the build an equilibrium model of commodity markets in which speculators are capital constrained, and commodity producers have hedging demands for commodity futures. Increases in producers' hedging demand or speculators' capital constraints increase hedging costs via price-pressure on futures. These in turn affect producers' equilibrium hedging and supply decision inducing a link between a financial friction in the futures market and the commodity spot prices. Consistent with the model, measures of producers' propensity to hedge forecasts futures returns and spot prices in oil and gas market data from 1979 to 2010. The component of the commodity futures risk premium associated with producer hedging demand rises when speculative activity reduces. We conclude that limits to financial arbitrage generate limits to hedging by producers, and affect equilibrium commodity supply and prices.

Jose SaulLizondo (2014). Described in the article "Foreign exchange futures prices under fixed exchange rates", that the paper develops three models for the determination of foreign exchange futures prices under fixed exchange rates and expectations of devaluation. These models show that certain characteristics of futures prices behavior that have been used as proof of inefficiency may be present even if the market is efficient. They also have several implications that are consistent with the observed behavior of Mexican Pesos futures prices. The gold reacts positively during market turbulence and negatively during economic growth. Since it maintains its intrinsic value, gold is often referred to as a haven. When fears about the security of other investments such as equities and bonds rise, many flock to gold because of its highly liquid nature. However, since the U.S. economy has continued to show signs of growth and the Federal Reserve is speculating forthcoming monetary changes, the value of gold will surely fluctuate.

Ing-Haw Cheng and Wei Xiong, (2014). defined in the research article "Financialization of Commodity Markets", that the large inflow of investment capital to commodity futures markets in the past decade has generated a heated debate about whether financialization distorts commodity prices. Rather than focusing on the opposing views concerning whether investment flows caused a price bubble, we critically review academic studies through the perspective of how financial investors affect risk sharing and information discovery in commodity markets. We argue that financialization has substantially changed commodity markets through these mechanisms.

Paul J. Seguin (2014). Described in article "Futures-Trading Activity and Stock Price Volatility" that the greater futures-trading activity (volume and open interest) is associated with greater equity volatility. We partition each trading activity series into expected and unexpected components, and document that while equity volatility covaries positively with unexpected futures-trading volume, it is negatively related to forecastable futures-trading activity. Further, though futures-trading activity is systematically related to the futures contract life cycle, we find no evidence of a relation between the futures life cycle and spot equity volatility. These findings are consistent with theories predicting that active futures markets enhance the liquidity and depth of the equity markets.

Hau Le Longab and Marc J. K. (2014). Examined in the article "Gold as a Hedge against Inflation: The Vietnamese Case" that the inflation-hedging properties of gold in Vietnam, reaching formidable records in 1980s-1990s. Consistent with conventional belief, we find that gold provides a complete hedge against both the ex post and ex ante inflation. In addition, its return is positively related to unexpected inflation, although the statistical evidence does not strongly support this. However, in general, we cannot reject that gold does provide a complete hedge against inflation. Furthermore, our findings support the Fisher hypothesis that nominal gold returns move in a one-for-one correspondence with expected inflation. The study has implications for both investors and government.

Piyamas Chaihetphon (2014). Defoned in the article "Gold Price discovery in the Indian", that the price discovery process of the nascent gold futures contracts in the Multi Commodity Exchange of India (MCX) over the period 2003 to 2007. The study employs vector error correction models (VECMs) to show that futures prices of both standard and mini contracts lead spot price. We find that mini contracts contribute to over 30% of price discovery in gold futures trade even though they account for only 2% of trading value on the MCX. Our finding reveals that trades initiated in mini contracts are much more informative than what the size of their market share of volume suggests.

Carl Ackermann and Richard McEnally (2014). Defined in the article "The Performance of Hedge Funds: Risk, Return, and Incentives", that the Hedge funds display several interesting characteristics that may influence performance, including: flexible investment strategies, strong managerial incentives, substantial managerial investment, sophisticated investors, and limited government oversight. Using a large sample of hedge fund data from 1988–1995, we find that hedge funds consistently outperform mutual funds, but not standard market indices. Hedge funds, however, are more volatile than both mutual funds and market indices. Incentive fees explain some of the higher performance, but not the increased total risk. The impact of six data-conditioning biases is explored. We find evidence that positive and negative survival-related biases offset each other.

Dipak Ghosh (2014). Described in the article "Gold as an Inflation Hedge" that the paper attempts to reconcile an apparent contradiction between short-run and long-run movements in the price of gold. The theoretical model suggests a set of conditions under which the price of gold rises over time at the general rate of inflation and hence be an effective hedge against inflation. The model also demonstrates that short-run changes in the gold lease rate, the real interest rate, convenience yield, default risk, the covariance of gold returns with other assets and the dollar/world exchange rate can disturb this equilibrium relationship and generate short-run price volatility. Using monthly gold price data (1976–1999), and co-integration regression techniques, an empirical analysis confirms the central hypotheses of the theoretical model.

Christian Pierdzioch and Sebastian Rohloff (2014). Disclosed in the article "On the efficiency of the gold market: Results of a real-time forecasting approach" that the real-time forecasting approach, we study whether publicly available information on a large set of financial and macroeconomic variables help in forecasting out-of-sample monthly excess returns on investing in gold. The real-time forecasting approach accounts for the fact that an investor must reach an investment decision in real time under uncertainty concerning the optimal forecasting model. The real-time forecasting approach also accounts for the possibility that the optimal forecasting model may change over time. We account for transaction costs and show that using forecasts implied by the real-time forecasting approach to set up a simple trading rule does not necessarily lead to a superior performance relative to a buy-and-hold strategy, implying that the gold market is informationally efficient with respect to the predictor variables that we study in this research.

Richard and Sundaresan (2014) described in the article "Comment: Investor demand and spot commodity prices", that the hedger can do two things for minimizing the risk namely first being either can square off the position at the time where he can face minimum risk or can gain profit as bonus if he has no margin left in respect of time i.e. if he has to buy or sell the gold for fulfilling the commitments on or before the expiry date of his future contract only, or the next can be rolling over the position, if there is still some time in fulfilling the commitments i.e. can buy/sell another far month contract for minimizing the risk, according to the movement of Basis and market.

Jesse Emspak, (2014) analysed in the article "What Moves Gold Prices? Why?" that the price of gold is moved by a combination of supply, demand and investor behavior. That seems simple enough, but the way those factors work together is sometimes counterintuitive. Many investors, for example, think of gold as an inflation hedge. That has some common sense plausibility paper money loses value as more is printed. But the supply of gold is relatively constant. As it happens mining doesn't add much year to year. When the Great Recession hit, gold prices rose. But gold was already rising up until the beginning of 2008, getting near $1,000 an ounce before falling under the $800 level and then bouncing back up and rising as the stock markets bottomed out. That said, gold prices kept rising even as the economy recovered.

Cox, Ingersoll and Ross (2015). Examine in the article "The relationship between spot and futures prices: An empirical analysis" that the "Despite the steep growth in demand, the Chinese gold market will continue to expand, irrespective of short-term blips in the economy. The private sector demand for gold in China is set to increase from the current level of 1,132 tons per year to at least 1,350 tons by 2013," the report said. In addition to a growing middle class, rising real incomes, a deepening pool of private savings and rapid urbanization across China suggest that the outlook for gold jewelry and investment demand in the next four years will remain strong, the report added. But China does not have a big influence on gold pricing despite the astonishing increase in gold demand.

Dilip Kumar Jha- (2015) examined in the article "Gold de-hedging at 9% in June quarter: Society General, Mumbai September 24, 2015 Business Standard" that the major indication for a rebound in gold price this year, global producers have squared off their long positions in commodity exchanges. Consequently, global miners reported 9 per cent decline in gold hedge in the second quarter of the current calendar year. A Societe General study conducted by Thomson Reuters GFMS titled "Global Hedge Book

Analysis 2Q '15" reported hedging in the overall gold holding of producers at 5.69 million oz (177 tonnes) for the quarter ended June 2015, a decline of 0.54 million oz (17 tonnes) from the previous quarter. This means, global gold producers de-hedged (squared off or abstained from hedging) of their positions amid fear of an upsurge in prices. "Gold miners normally hedge on fears of declining prices to protect their margins from further fall.

Ding, Z., Granger, C.W.J., Engle, R.F., (2015). Analyse in the article "Long memory property of stock market returns and a new model" that the number of autoregressive conditional heteroskedasticity (ARCH) and GARCH models are nested within the APGARCH model. To estimate the goodness of fit of each model, likelihood ratio tests are used to assess the significance of each model and provide the best fit for the data. The results suggest that APGARCH model provides the most adequate description for the data, with the inclusion of a GARCH term, free power term and unrestricted leverage effect term.

George Emir Morgan (2015). Examined in the article "Forward and futures pricing of treasury bills" that the recent literature on interest rate futures contracts applying both traditional futures and term structure theories. It is argued that an important characteristic of futures contracts has been ignored in most of the futures literature. By constructing a riskless arbitrage between implicit forward contracts and futures contracts, it is demonstrated that even in an efficient market the futures and forward prices will be different. The difference results because the `marking to the market' that is required on a futures contract implies that the course of interest rates is important to the pricing of interest rate futures contracts.

Trevir Nath (2015). Explain in the article "Why is Gold a Counter Cyclical Asset?" that the Worldwide, gold is seen as a valuable commodity with intrinsic value. Until 1934, the U.S. dollar was backed by gold, with notes redeemable in exchange for the precious metal. Today gold remains valuable for its rarity and ability to create jewelry and other beautiful objects. It's also an investment vehicle in the commodities market.

Like any commodity, gold has its ticker symbols, contract value and margin requirements. The investment is valued by supply and demand mainly speculative demand. However, unlike other commodities, the value of gold is less affected by consumption and largely influenced by the status of the economy.

Dietrich Domanski and Alexandra Heath (2015). Described in the article "Financial Investors and Commodity Markets" that the commodities have attracted considerable interest as a financial investment in recent years. This article discusses the factors behind their growing appeal and assesses the extent to which market characteristics, such as price volatility, have changed as a result. The feature concludes that commodity markets have become more like financial markets in terms of the motivations and strategies of participants, but that the physical characteristics of commodity markets are still important.

Kevin A. McCabe and Stephen J. Rassenti (2015). Described in the article "Designing a Uniform-Price Double Auction: An Experimental Evaluation" that the alternative form of auction which allows continuous orders but executes contracts in real time as in a call market. Since contracts are executed at a single point in time, there is one market price. This motivates the name of the proposed auction: The Uniform-Price Double Auction (UPDA). UPDA is conceptually equivalent to a clearinghouse institution reported in Friedman, although there are some implementational differences. The chapter explores that the technology of laboratory experimentation can facilitate the interplay between the evaluation and modification of proposed new exchange institutions before field implementation. It compares the behavior of UPDA with double auctions (DA) and double Dutch (DD). The parametric environment chosen to motivate subjects in DA experiments allows one to make many "independent" observations on the same basic market game. Since both prices and relative bargaining strengths are randomly fluctuating, it becomes very difficult for subjects to strategize on the basis of knowledge of the environment.

Long Yu (2015). Described in the article "Visibility graph network analysis of gold price time series", that the mapping time series into a visibility graph network, the characteristics of the gold price time series and return temporal series, and the mechanism underlying the gold price fluctuation have been explored from the perspective of complex network theory. The network degree distribution characters, which change from power law to exponent law when the series was shuffled from original sequence, and the average path length characters, which change from into as the sequence was shuffled, demonstrate that price series and return series are both long-rang dependent fractal series. The relations of Hurst exponent to the power-law exponent of degree distribution demonstrate that the logarithmic price series is a fractal Brownian series and the logarithmic return series is a fractal Gaussian series.

Jean Folger (2016). Examined in the article "The trends of Price of Gold?" that the Gold is sought after not only for investment purposes and a strong jewelry market, but it is also used in the manufacturing of certain electronic and medical devices. Gold (as of March, 2011) was around $1,420 per ounce and making record highs. What factors drive the price of this precious metal? Central banks hold paper currencies and gold in reserve. The World Gold Council has stated that central banks have recently begun buying more gold than they are selling, the first time this has happened in decades. As the central banks diversify their monetary reserves - away from the paper currencies they've accumulated and into gold - the price of gold rises. Many of the world's nations have reserves that are composed primarily of gold, including the United States, Germany, Italy, France, Portugal, Greece and the Euro area.

World Gold Council Report (2016) states in the article "Investors should consider doubling their gold allocations amid negative interest rates- Market Update: Gold in a world of negative interest rates - Published on 31st March 2016" that the new and unprecedented phase in monetary policy. Central banks in Europe and Japan have now implemented Negative Interest Rate Policies (NIRP) to counteract deflationary pressures and, in some cases, currency appreciation. Amid higher market uncertainty, the price of gold is up by 16% year-to-date – in part due to NIRP. Investors, including central bank managers, should assess the implications of holding bonds with negative return expectations on portfolio composition and risk management. Analysis shows that, firstly, Gold returns in periods of low rates are historically twice as high as their long-run average and secondly, Investors may benefit from increasing their gold holdings up to 2.5 times, depending on the asset mix, even under conservative assumptions for gold.

Pravin Palande (2016) described in the article "investing in gold is completely going out of fashion" that the t a time when investing in gold is completely going out of fashion, Asia Index, a joint venture between S&P Dow Jones Indices and BSE, launched an index which is a combination of equities and gold. Aptly named, the S&P BSE Sensex Gold Hedged Index and S&P Dynamic Gold Hedged Index is created with an idea to hedge against a falling rupee than a falling market itself. The hedged index is designed to create a strategy which is long the S&P BSE Sensex and hedged against changes in the Indian rupee versus gold. "This is one index that we are launching almost simultaneously in the USA and India. The idea is to create new products for investors across countries. Over the last ten years, both gold and equity have given positive returns at 13 percent and 10 percent respectively, and the correlation between the two asset classes over the last ten years is at a -0.0407, which is considered to be significant to create a hedged index.

Stephen D. Simpson, (2016). Described in the article "How Much Disaster Can Gold Hedge?" that the Gold has had a special hold on the minds of many investors for centuries, if not millennia, offering the promise of being the one asset that will never go to zero, and the one medium of exchange that other people will always accept in trade. While these notions are basically true, investors would do well to consider just how much disaster they can really hedge by buying gold. Whenever it is time to debate the merits of gold, it is only a matter of time before someone mentions the iffy correlation between gold and inflation. The history of gold versus inflation looks a lot like a bungee cord - years and years go by and nothing seems to be happening, until there's a point of release and the price of gold rockets up.

Dalton Barker (2016). Examined in the article "Gold market experiences minor loss, dollar strengthens" that the Gold futures escaped a major selloff Friday in the US despite signs that American labour market is heading for its eighth year of expansion. Gold for August delivery on the Comex division of the New York Mercantile Exchange was last down $2.10 or 0.2 percent at $1,360.0 per ounce. Trade has ranged from $1,336.30 to $1,371.80. The precious metal initially dropped over 1.5 percent on the release of the latest June employment report, which showed 287,000 Americans entered the labour market – far exceeding expectations of 174,000. Average hourly earnings period ticked up 0.1 percent, below the forecast 0.2 percent. Though the unemployment rate rose to 4.9 percent from 4.8, the uptick was due mostly from an increase in the labour participation rate. The news settled equity markets and reignited optimism that the US economy was strengthening even as concerns exist over the health of the European Union and Chinese economy.

Sham Gad (2016). Described in the article "Why and under which situation the Gold Price Matters?" that the topic of investing in gold came to the forefront of many investors' minds during the 2008-2009 recession. The most obvious reason for this was due to the rise in the price of gold. Market watchers love to sensationalize any stock or asset class that is experiencing a rise in price as the next possible investment to latch on to. Yet the rise in the price of gold happened largely due to people buying physical gold or betting on the metal through various investment options, such as ETFs or gold miner stocks. The Great Recession of 2008 is set to have profound effects on our economic system for decades to come. This was also seen after the UK voted to leave the EU in 2016, when gold prices soared as Britain's economic future was deemed highly uncertain. Before jumping on the gold bandwagon, first examine reasons why investing in gold holds fundamental problems.

Noble DraKoln (2016) defined in the article "The Gold Showdown: ETFs Vs. Futures?" that the first exchange-traded fund (ETF) specifically developed to track the price of gold was introduced in the United States. It was touted as an inexpensive alternative to owning physical gold or buying gold futures, and since its introduction,

ETFs have become a widely accepted alternative. Many investors look to certain gold-specific ETFs as a convenient and exciting way to participate in gold without having to be exposed to the risks of physically purchasing bullion or gaining a practical understanding on how gold futures operate. However, what many investors fail to realize is that the price to trade ETFs that track gold may exceed their convenience, and that trading gold future contracts may be a better alternative under the right circumstances. In this article, we'll explore whether it's better to invest in gold ETFs or to go with the more traditional gold futures. For more sophisticated investors, or those with investing capital that exceeds a few hundred dollars, there are significant drawbacks to investing in gold-specific ETFs that go beyond the day-to-day fluctuation of gold prices.

Bradford Cornell and Mrc R. Reinganum (2017). Described in the article "Forward and Futures Prices: Evidence from the Foreign Exchange Markets", that the Empirical studies of the Treasury Bill markets have revealed substantial differences between the futures price and the implied forward price. These differences have been attributed to taxes, transaction costs, and the settling up procedure employed in the futures market. This paper examines the forward and futures prices in foreign exchange in an attempt to distinguish between the competing explanations. The conclusion Erb and Harvey made, though, was that the purchasing power of gold stayed pretty constant. It also seems unrelated to the current price. If you're looking at gold prices, it's probably a good idea to look at how well the economies of certain countries are doing. As economic conditions worsen the price will (usually) rise. Gold is a commodity that isn't tied to anything else, so it makes a good diversifier in a portfolio in small doses.

Elizabeth Ferry (2018). Analysed in the article "Gold prices as material-social actors: The case of the London Gold Fix", that the opinion piece, drawn from a larger research project on market perceptions of physical gold and gold derivatives, argues that scholars of extractive resources have paid little attention to the pragmatics of prices or looked at prices as material-social actors in their own right. Drawing on literature from the Social Studies of Finance, this essay looks at the global benchmark gold price (formerly the London Gold Fix, now the LBMA London Gold Price) to see how its material and semiotic embeddedness affects its connections to other aspects of gold investment and gold mining.

Andrew W. Lo (2018). Described in the article "Risk Management for Hedge Funds: Introduction and Overview" that the risk management has been a well-plowed field in financial modeling for more than two decades, traditional risk management tools such as mean–variance analysis, beta, and Value-at-Risk do not capture many of the risk exposures of hedge-fund investments. The review several unique aspects of risk management for hedge funds survivorship bias, dynamic risk analytics, liquidity, and nonlinearities and provide examples that illustrate their potential importance to hedge-fund managers and investors. I propose a research agenda for developing a new set of risk analytics specifically designed for hedge-fund investments, with the ultimate goal of creating risk transparency without compromising the proprietary nature of hedge-fund investment strategies.

Kenneth R. French (2018). Examined in the article "A comparison of futures and forward prices" that the relation between futures and forward prices for copper and silver. There are significant differences between these prices. The average differences are generally consistent with the predictions of the futures and forward price models. However, these models are not helpful in describing intra-sample variations in the futures-forward price differences. This failure is apparently caused by measurement errors in both the price differences and in the explanatory variables. The World Gold Council's 2014 figures show that total demand was 3,923.7 metric tons, but only 389 tons was for the tech sector. The rest was investment at 904.6 tons and jewelry at 2,152.9 tons. Even though in countries like India and China gold can act as a store of value, the people that buy it there don't regularly trade it (few pay for a washing machine by handing over a gold bracelet).

Laurence E. Blose and Joseph C. P. Shieh (2018). Analysed in the article "The impact of gold price on the value of gold mining stock" that the value of a gold mine is shown to be a function of the return on gold, production costs, the level of gold reserves, and the proportion of assets unrelated to gold price risk. Assuming that forward gold prices are the market's unbiased expectations of future spot prices, a model is derived that estimates the theoretical gold price elasticity of gold mining stock. The model shows that if a company's primary business is gold mining, the gold price elasticity of the company's stock is greater than one. Using monthly data over the ten year period 1981 through 1990, the model is tested for a sample of 23 publicly traded gold mining companies.

Joscha Beckmannal and Robert Czudaj (2018). Examined in the article "Gold as an inflation hedge in a time-varying coefficient framework" that the question whether gold provides the ability of hedging against inflation from a new perspective. Using data for four major economies, namely the USA, the UK, the Euro Area, and Japan, we allow for nonlinearity and discriminate between long-run and time-varying short-run dynamics. Thus, we conduct a Markov-switching vector error correction model (MS-VECM) approach for a sample period ranging from January 1970 to December 2011. Our main findings are threefold: first, we show that gold is partially able to hedge future inflation in the long-run and this ability is stronger for the USA and the UK compared to Japan and the Euro Area. In addition, the adjustment of the general price level is characterized by regime-dependence, implying that the usefulness of gold as an inflation hedge for investors crucially depends on the time horizon. Finally, one regime approximately accounts for times of turbulence while the other roughly corresponds to 'normal times'.

Li Lili and Diao Chengmei (2018). Described in the article "Research of the Influence of Macro-Economic Factors on the Price of Gold" that the dynamics of gold prices in the Gold Exchange in NEW YORK using a dataset that includes global macroeconomic indicators, financial market indices, quantities and prices of energy products. We extract common factors from the panel data series and estimate a Factor-Augmented Vector Auto-regression for gold prices. It shows that a factor correlated to purely financial developments contributes to the model performance, in addition to factors related to gold reserves and energy prices. This paper has two main contributions. First, all factors influencing the gold market have been classified into three groups, that is, gold reserve and prices of energy products, financial market indices, global macroeconomic indicators. We can see that the effect of financial market indices and macroeconomic indicators to gold price is negative, the effect of gold reserve and prices of energy product to gold price is positive. Second, we apply the FAVAR model to analysis factors influencing gold price and the trend of gold price.

Raj Aggarwalal and Brian M. Lucey (2018). Examined in the article "Psychological barriers in gold prices?" that the paper examines for the first time the existence of psychological barriers in a variety of daily and intra-day gold price series. This paper uses a number of statistical procedures and presents evidence of psychological barriers in gold prices. We document that prices in round numbers act as barriers with important effects on the conditional mean and variance of the gold price series around psychological barriers. During times of economic uncertainty and when the dollar is weak, however, people prefer to invest in gold, through vehicles such as gold funds or coins. In 2017, jewelry accounted for approximately 54% percent of gold demand, which totaled 3,812 tonnes, according to the World Gold Council and The London Bullion Market Association. India, China and the United States are the largest consumers of gold for jewelry in terms of volume.

Werner Kristjan and Marcel C. Minutolo (2018). Analysed in the article "Gold price volatility: A forecasting approach using the Artificial Neural Network" that the most used methods to forecast price volatility is the generalized autoregressive conditional heteroskedasticity model. Nonetheless, the errors in prediction using this approach are often quite high. Hence, continued research is conducted to improve forecasting models employing a variety of techniques. In this paper, we extend the field of expert systems, forecasting, and model by applying an Artificial Neural Network (ANN). Gold prices can be affected by the basic theory of supply and demand: as demand for consumer goods such as jewelry and electronics increase, the cost of gold can rise. During times of economic uncertainty, as seen during the recession more people turn to investing in gold because of its enduring value. Gold is often considered a "safe haven" for investors during uncertain times.

RESEARCH GAP

Even though, there are number of research studies related to "Bullion", "Bullion Market", "Gold Futures", "Hedging", "Risk" and "Risk Management", they are mostly in the context of companies operating in developed economies. There are very few research studies that focus on "Dimensions of Gold Futures with special reference to Bullion Market" and also pertain to "Risks in Investing Gold". Other prominent reasons for taking up the present study are the few numbers of comprehensive studies on "Dimensions of Gold Futures with special reference to Bullion Market" in Indian context in general and "Indian Bullion Market" in particular as depicted by the literature review, and therefore, the research gap.

Hence to conclude, a need was felt to take up a comprehensive study of dimensions of gold futures which aims at covering hidden insights with respective factors influencing the volatility in the bullion market with respect to gold.

CHAPTER - 4

RESEARCH METHODOLOGY

4.1 TITLE OF THE STUDY

DIMENSIONS OF COMMODITY FUTURES - A STUDY WITH SPECIAL REFERENCE TO BULLION MARKET

4.2 STATEMENT OF THE PROBLEM

Investing in the bullion market doesn't derive without risk due to volatility in the bullion market. A market crash could crush this investment's performance, even if the quality of the investment remains the same since investments also follow trends. The various types of risks associated with investing in bullion market are market risk, default risk, Inflation risk, interest rate risk, financial risk, political risk, liquidity risk and emotional risk. The market mood is influenced by the political climate in the country. Combating all these types of risks is a major challenge.

The bullion market can be a great thing, but both the buyers and Dealers to the future contract must first understand the risks and their risk tolerance before putting their money to work in the market. An ailing economy puts all gold reserves at risk, no matter the management team or the goodwill strength. It is believed that inflation is a much bigger investment risk that most investor ever recognizes. It is challenge for the investors and gold seller to create a position in the market without encountering difficulties and problems. Difficulties arise in various areas of trade like arrangement of finance, recovery of debts, rejection of a consignment, change in government policies, labour unrest and many such unexpected situations.

Research Issues and Research Questions

- The research issues related to the volatility in the bullion market with respect to gold.
- The various risks factors that are to be addressed in view of the volatility.
- What is the hedging mechanism to counter various risks associated with volatility?

- What are the dimensions of commodity futures of bullion market of select Western markets with India?

4.3 OBJECTIVES

Based on the above statement of problems, the following objectives were derived:

- To study and understand the volatility in the bullion market with respect to gold.
- To identify various risks factors that are to be addressed in view of the volatility.
- To examine the hedging mechanism to counter various risks associated with volatility.
- To compare and contrast the dimensions of commodity futures of bullion market of select Western markets with India.
- To develop a suggestive framework model based on the study.

4.4 SCOPE OF THE STUDY

The scope of the study is outlined through the following points:

(i) The scope of the study is limited to the Indian Bullion Market represented by Dimensions of Gold Futures especially in Karnataka State.

(ii) The research was restricted to the "Regular Investors of Gold Futures", "Gold Dealers" and "Stock Brokers" which are applicable to commonly observing Risks in Investing Gold such as "Price Risk", "Exchange Rate Risk", "Bankruptcy of Bank", "Trading Interruptions", "Operational Risk", "Identity Theft", "Insurance Exclusions", and "Termination of Gold Republic".

(iii) "Dimensions of Gold Futures with special reference to Bullion Market" is also applicable to commonly identifying factors influencing the volatility in the bullion market with respect to gold such as "Global Crisis", "Inflation Rate", "Value of the U.S. Dollar", "Interest Rates", "Consumption of Gold", "Recession in world market", "Gold demand and supply" and "REPO Rate".

(iv) The aim of the research is to find the facts and opinions of the investors in gold future trading so as to find the buoyancy for futures. The study also attempts to seek the opinion of investors future trading used as a hedging measure in risk management and explain the practical approach for hedging risk owing to the difference in the environmental factors of different countries such as UK, USA, India etc. This study covers investors from BSE, NSE, NASDAQ, LSE, SGX.

4.5 HYPOTHESIS

Based on the objectives of the study, following hypotheses were formulated to facilitate the purposeful research methodology:

H_{01}: Eight Factors together do not influence the functional dimension.

Or,

Mathematically, ***H_{01}***: *[The influence of eight factors on functional dimension] = 0*

H_{02}: Eight Factors together do not influence the demographic dimension.

Or,

Mathematically, ***H_{02}***: *[The influence of eight factors on demographic dimension] = 0*

H_{03}: Eight Factors together do not influence the opportunity dimension.

Or,

Mathematically, ***H_{03}***: *[The influence of eight factors on opportunity dimension] = 0*

H_{04}: The Eight Factors together do not influence the financial dimension.

Or,

Mathematically, ***H_{04}***: *[The influence of eight factors on financial dimension] = 0*

4.6 OPERATIONAL DEFINITION OF CONCEPTS

4.6.1 Functional Dimension

The functional dimension captures the effects of the volatility in the bullion market in the form of impurity while making and designing jewelry especially in Industrial Usage and Individual Usage.

4.6.2 Demographic Dimension

This dimension captures the effects of the volatility in the bullion market in the form of income level and marital status with reference to Degree of Savings and Long term investment plan.

4.6.3 Opportunity Dimension

This dimension captures the effects of the volatility in the bullion market with respect to resale value and Investment during times of economic instability, volatile commodity markets.

4.6.4 Financial Dimension

This dimension captures the effects of the volatility in the bullion market in the form of "Liquidating gold through the dealer" and "Storing and protecting gold".

4.6.5 Individual Investor

Individual investors are the general public, take decisions regarding long term investment in bullion market.

4.6.6 Gold Dealer

Gold dealers make money on buying gold from the public. Many gold dealers are simply marketing companies, which mean they facilitate the trades but do not keep inventory on hand. When you sell your gold to a gold dealer, that dealer is likely going to sell those same metals to a large-scale depository or wholesaler.

4.6.7 Stock Broker

Stock broker is a regulated professional individual, usually associated with a brokerage firm or broker-dealer, who buys and sells stocks and other securities for both retail and institutional clients through a stock exchange or over the counter in return for a fee or commission.

4.6.8 Bullion

Bullion is gold, silver, or other precious metals in the form of bars or ingots. Bullion is used for trade on a market. The value of bullion is determined by the value of its precious metals content which is defined by its purity and frame.

4.6.9 Bullion Market

Bullion market is a market where traders trade in precious metals like gold and silver. This is a place where exchanges of gold and silver take place over the counter and in the futures market. Trading in bullions market is open 24 hours. Bullion markets exist across the globe and most of the transactions take place through electronic means or by phone.

4.7 METHODOLOGY

The research methodology consisted of identification of key categories of factors and subsequently the constituent factors and dimensions under each category through three iteration Delphi Technique wherein the Delphi panel consisted 10 experts having diverse background. Taking these inputs and purposeful contemplation on the part of the researcher the "constructs" necessary for the questionnaire were formulated. Research Methodology is the combination of methods of data collection and methods of data analysis after Research Design.

4.7.1 Instruments of the Research Study

Various instruments i.e., Delphi Technique, Questionnaire Design and Factor Analysis were employed. At first all the relevant problems and prospects were identified through Delphi Techniques, Questionnaire was designed based on the variables related to those problems and prospects were confirmed by Factor Analysis.

4.7.1.1 Utilize of Delphi Technique

At first 10 experts were selected from diverse background and built Delphi Panel. The experts were asked about their opinion regarding "Factors influencing the volatility" and "Dimensions of Gold Futures" related to their organization. In the first attempt the experts were unseen about the main concept and they have given some opinions, the researcher has taken it consideration the commonality of the opinions. At the second attempt, the same experts were asked for their opinions those who have given their opinions previously. In this attempt the experts have identified some common patterns that were further refined with the consideration of previous communality.

Total 10 experts were interviewed and collected the opinion regarding Factors influencing the volatility. Under the first iteration, total 45 items were identified related to different problems and history. The result from the first attempt found that the normality not within agreeable limits.

Under the second Iteration, causes and history factors merged and items are shown reduced from 45 to 27. The mean percentage agreement became 60.70%, that means the level of normality may be improved.

Under the third Iteration, the items were further filtered and reduced from 27 to 22 and 8 problems arrived at. The mean percentage agreement became 82.70%, that means the level of normality well within limits. When the Mean % Agreement cross 70% can be accepted, then the factors influencing the volatility have identified and validate with the help of Mean % Aggregate value was 82.7%.

Delphi Technique is employed to identify the prospects of export marketing of readymade garments. Total 10 experts were interviewed and collected the opinion regarding prospects of export marketing. As per experts opinion 18 items were identified related to different prospects and history.

The result from the first attempt found that the normality not within agreeable limits.

The summary of second Iteration shows the reduced items from 18 to 14 with the merged of effect factors and motivational factors. The mean percentage agreement became 66.70%, that means the level of normality may be improved.

The summary of third Iteration shows the reduced items from 14 to 8 with the four (4) widely observed Dimensions of Gold Futures. The mean percentage agreement became 89.70% that means the level of normality well within limits.

4.7.1.2 Designing and Developing of Questionnaire

After identifying three categories of problems and prospects by using Delphi Technique, the questionnaire design was initiated. The statements were arrived by sitting with my guide for some days. The statements were further consulted by some experts and confirmed by using the Pilot Study of 80 respondents and finally the questionnaire was designed. Following steps taken into consideration while design and develop of questionnaire:-

Step-1: Constructs Formulation

The construct was formulated by considering the keyword "Factors influencing the volatility". This terminology is analyzed in details (Appendix-2) to identify and confirm various factors. Constructs were formulated by arranging of constituent aspects that contribute to the phenomenon of getting information reading Factors influencing the volatility.

Step-2: Formation of Statements

The statement is the sentence that states the main concept about research study. The statements reflect the experts' opinion that the researcher present in a reader friendly manner. The questions were designed in questionnaire with the help of statements. The final questions were written in questionnaire with proper serial numbers which were mentioned after writing statement.

Step-4: Defining of Problems and Prospects

Various influencing factors of volatilities are: "Global Crisis", "Inflation Rate", "Value of the U.S. Dollar", "Interest Rates", "Consumption of Gold", "Recession in world market", "Gold demand and supply" and "REPO Rate".

Various commonly identifying dimensions are: "Functional Dimension", "Demographic Dimension", "Opportunity Dimension" and "Financial Dimension"

Step-4: Pilot Study

Pilot study was employed to refine and re-refine the questionnaire. Firstly the pilot survey was conducted on a small sample size of 10 respondents, before conducting the full-fledged survey. This was done to know the respondents clarity of questions in questionnaire, to avoid further problems of interpretation by respondents. All the alterations were incorporated after the feedback was received. The alterations were regarding clarity, shape, consistency and quality of questions. Finally, the pilot survey was conducted on a sample size of 80 respondents which were distributed 40 among Investors of Gold Futures, 20 among Gold Dealers and 20 among Stock Brokers. To ensure the validity and reliability of data collected before the further analysis, the test of validity and reliability was applied.

Step-5: Validity and Reliability Test

Validity is the degree to be scaled of measuring what it is intent to the questionnaire. The scale is measuring some impression regarding Dimensions of Gold Futures with special reference to Bullion Market.

In this research study the concurrent validity test is employed and shown in details in (Appendix). The concurrent validity is a method of calculating validity with comparable samples. Reliability is the degree to which scale provide the repeated result from the same type of respondents. Cronbach's Alpha is employed for Reliability test (Appendix). Comparable to Reliability Test the Validity Test is more important because it measures what it is to be measured and then only the question of repeatability comes. Cronbach's Alpha was calculated to measure the internal consistency reliability of the instrument.

The reliability of scales used in this study was calculated by Cronbach's coefficient alpha and normally it ranges between 0 and 1. All constructs obtained an acceptable level of a coefficient alpha above 0.6, indicating the scales used in this study were reliable.

4.7.1.3 Utilize of Factor Analysis

Factor analysis is employed to confirm the factors which were identified through Delphi Technique. Factor analysis is applied as a data reduction or structure detection method. Factor analysis is the technique that shows how we have reduced 22 variables to 8 variables. Factor Analysis was carried out by principle component analysis where in the 8 principle components were involved along with VARIMAX rotation.

4.7.2 Research Design

The research questions and consequently the research objectives call for a hybrid research design which is a combination of descriptive, survey and Analytical research design carried-out without manipulation of the prevailing conditions in the form of empirical research. Here the responses with respect to Dimensions of Gold Futures with special reference to Bullion Market were gathered by employing stratified random sampling.

4.7.3 Variables Definitions

Once the construct was formulated, the researcher has identified the variables. Through Delphi technique the Factors of volatility and Dimensions of Gold Futures were identified. The Individual Investor, Gold Dealers and Stock Brokers have given their valuable opinion regarding Factors of volatility and Dimensions of Gold Futures. Each category further classified into several variables that were confirmed through factor analysis.

Variables have defined by considering the technical words of Research Title and various Objectives. The variables were categorized into independent variables and dependent variables. Independent variables are the variables that are changed or controlled in a scientific experiment to test the effects on the dependent variable. Dependent variables are the variables being tested and measured in a scientific experiment. In the present research study the "Factors influencing the volatility in the bullion market" are the independent variables and "Dimensions of Gold Futures" are the dependent variables.

4.7.4 Type of Research Methods used

4.7.4.1 Descriptive Research Method

Descriptive research method is used to describe various aspects of the phenomenon. In its popular format, descriptive research is used to describe characteristics and/or behaviour of sample population. The present study considers the historical data to fulfil the requirements of the objectives, the descript research method is implemented for the same reason.

4.7.4.2 Survey Research Method

Survey research is one of the most important areas of measurement in applied social research. The broad area of survey research encompasses any measurement procedures that involve asking questions of respondents. The questionnaire has prepared and collected data from the selected respondents, the survey research method consider as the valid decision for the present research study.

4.7.4.3 Analytical Research Method

Analytical Method is a generic process combining the power of the Scientific Method with the use of formal process to solve any type of problem. The issues and problems of the present study keep on changing time to time and situation to situation, so get in depth understanding and productive solutions the analytical research method has implemented.

4.7.5 Sampling

After identifying the variables, the questionnaire has designed to collect required data from the reliable and responsive representative of entire population. Sample design is a means of structuring the sample to select a subset of units from a target population for the purpose of collecting required information. This information is used to draw inferences about the population as a whole. The respondents were ensured by conducting the survey at Bangalore among Investors of Gold Futures, Gold Dealers and Stock Brokers. This enabled a fair degree of representation of the Indian context related to Factors influencing volatility and Dimensions of Gold Futures. In order to get the picture about reality the representations have selected from all the three categories of respondents.

Population

Population is the sum total of all the individuals who have definite characteristics and are of curiosity to a researcher. The population related to the present research study included the Investors of Gold Futures, Gold Dealers and Stock Brokers.

Universe - All gold stocks traded in BSE, NSE, NASDAQ, London stock exchange, Singapore stock exchange (SGX).

- All parties to future contracts in the commodity-gold
- All stock broking companies in relation to commodity futures-gold

Table 4.1 Composition of Sample Size

Sl. No	Category of Respondents	Sample Size	Sampling Technique Used
1	Investors in Gold Futures	392/400	Convenience Sampling
2	Gold Dealers	184/200	Convenience Sampling
3	Stock Brokers	54/100	Convenience Sampling
	Total	630/700	

Semi-structured interview schedules were prepared for improving the quality of data. The data were considered based on expert opinions regarding the impact of Factors influencing volatility and Dimensions of Gold Futures. Through the interview schedule, the data were collected from the several managerial people. Semi-structured interview schedules were prepared separately for Investors of Gold Futures, Gold Dealers and Stock Brokers. Out of total 630 samples, 315 were randomly picked up for semi-structured interviews.

4.7.6 Data Collection

The present research study is based on data collected from both primary as well as secondary sources. Collection of primary data is done through the questionnaire, semi-structured interview schedule and observation methods. Secondary data was collected from published reports of the business magazines, newspapers, and company websites and "Bullion", "Bullion Market", "Gold Futures", "Hedging", "Risk" and "Risk Management" in their titles related literature.

4.7.6.1 Primary Data Collection

The present research is empirical in nature and data are collected through experience and observation.

Tools of Primary Data Collection

Considering the nature of respondents, the following tools of collecting primary data were used. Tools for primary data collection involved structured and pilot study validated questionnaire, semi-structured interview schedules and observation methods. Questionnaire is the series of questions asked to the respective stakeholders to obtain statistically useful information related to the given topic. The interview schedule is prepared for collecting data. Observation method has employed to go for silent observation of Investors of Gold Futures and Stock Brokers.

Data has been gathered using questionnaire as a tool; which was designed based on the literature reviewed and interviews with experts in the field. The questionnaire was a structured one used after due validation and included both open ended and close ended questions to augment and supplement information needed for the study. Based on the title and objective of the study, the questionnaire contained 4 major parts to achieve the objectives of the research.

Part 1 –Demographic details on the basic information of the investors

Part 2 – Factors influencing the price movements in bullion market

Part 3 – The various aspects of profit model for the hedging strategy adopted by the investors.

Part 4 –The growth indicators of the bullion market and the challenges for growth

4.7.6.2 Secondary Data Collection

To get a picture about the context of the research questions, data was also collected from secondary sources such as business magazines, newspapers, company websites and Bullion Market functions related literature. The research could not complete until the researcher obtained supportive information through secondary sources. The researcher continuously kept in touch with secondary sources of data for verifying, comparing with primary data. It helps to make primary data collection more specific since with the help of secondary data, the researcher was able to make out what were the gaps and deficiencies and what additional information needs to be collected.

4.8 PLAN OF ANALYSIS

For the purpose of analysis of data, the researcher has used descriptive and inferential statistical tools and techniques which are as follows:

a) Descriptive statistics

In the present research study, descriptive statistics are used to describe the basic features of the data in a study. They provide simple summaries about the sample and the measures. Together with simple graphics analysis, they form the basis of virtually every quantitative analysis of data.

b) Inferential statistics

Inferential statistics are used to make inferences about populations using data drawn from the population. Instead of using the entire population to gather the data, the statistician will collect a sample or samples from the millions of residents and make inferences about the entire population using the sample.

4.9 LIMITATIONS OF THE STUDY

The research study is having few limitations which are given bellow:

- The study is confined to commodity futures of bullion market – gold only. The underlying assets for the study are gold stocks and its price movements.
- Findings of the study relate to the particular point of time which might change due to fluctuations in the environmental factors.
- Hedging is subjected to volatility in the price movements of the underlying asset.
- The study aims at maximizing objectivity. Subjectivity cannot be ruled out due to sampling errors.
- Certain critical information related to financial performance, cost of service per beneficiary was not considered as the respondents were not very forthcoming to divulge financial data easily.
- This study is conducted as an academic interest and suffers from time and cost constraints.

4.10 REFERENCE PERIOD

a) Secondary data is collected from 2013 to 2016

b) Primary data collected in the year 2013 to 2016

c) Research study commenced from August 2012 and completed in August 2018

4.11 CHAPTER SCHEME

Chapter - 1: Introduction to Bullion Market - An Overview

Bullion market is a market where traders trade in precious metals like gold and silver. This is a place where exchanges of gold and silver take place over the counter and in the futures market.

Trading in bullions market is open 24 hours. Bullion markets exist across the globe and most of the transactions take place through electronic means or by phone. First Chapter contains the basic introduction about bullion market, significance of Bullion Market, Bullion Market in the Indian Economy.

Chapter - 2: Hedging and Risk Management

Hedging is an insurance method for commodity traders, producers and end-users to cover themselves against negative price movements. The aim of this strategy is to restrict the losses that may arise due to unknown fluctuations in the investment prices and to lock the profits therein. Second Chapter contains the basic concept hedging, areas of hedging and their risks, classification of hedging, hedging strategies, gold hedge fund manager, gold hedge fund performance, advantages of hedging, disadvantages of hedging, describe the concept of risk and various risks in bullion market.

Chapter - 4: Review of Literature

In view of dynamic in nature it is required to study the theme in the practical world to arrive at the hidden patterns. The lack of a comprehensive study was done on Dimensions of Gold Futures with special reference to Bullion Market. Chapter 4 contains the Purpose of literature review, Comments by experts and Document review.

Chapter - 4: Research Methodology

Research methodology consists of identification of key categories of factors and subsequently the constituent factors under each category through three iteration Delphi Techniques. Taking these inputs and purposeful contemplation on the part of the researcher the "constructs" necessary for the questionnaire were formulated. This chapter contains the feasibility of the study, scope of the study, research gap, statement of problems, objectives of the study, hypotheses for the study, research design, validity and reliability test and limitations of the study.

Chapter - 5: Analysis and Interpretation

Analysis and interpretation of gold futures would be done with the help of statistical tools and techniques. The collected data were analyzed by employing the statistical techniques of Normality Testing, Coefficient of Variation (CV) and Multiple Regression Analysis to obtain the hidden patterns with respect to export marketing of readymade garments. The required analysis was done with the aid of Statistical Package for Social Sciences (SPSS) 20.0 Version. The variables were coded in SPSS and certain statistical methods were applied on the data to get the results which are analyzed.

Chapter - 6: Summary of Findings, Conclusion and Suggestions

In this chapter, the researcher has given the summary of conclusions by respecting each objective of the study and the major findings which are related to the extra effort for understanding the broad research area. Based on the study the Suggestions and Recommendations were listed. The key suggestions call for comparative studies between medium and small scale organizations, whereas the main recommendation highlights need to keep in mind the "core nature" of the export marketing of readymade garments.

References

The research study contains references which lists all the sources used or consulted in writing the entire thesis and is placed at the very end of the work. The complete extracts are arranged alphabetically by last name of the author. The researcher has applied American Psychological Association (APA) style to arrange references.

Appendices

Appendices include Questionnaire, Delphi Method, Factor Analysis, Semi-Structure Interview Schedule and Published Research Papers.

Hence to conclude, this chapter covers the statement of the problem, objectives and the scope of the study, hypotheses of the study, research methodology being used in the study, data collection ,limitation and chapter schemes indicating the outline of thesis.

CHAPTER - 5
DIMENSIONS OF COMMODITY FUTURES- A STUDY WITH SPECIAL REFERENCE TO BULLION MARKET: ANALYSIS AND INTERPRETATION

This chapter intends to accomplish the objectives of the study by holistically investigating "Dimensions of Gold Futures with special reference to Bullion Market". The collected data were arranged systematically with required tables. The arranged data were analyzed by employing the statistical techniques of Factor Analysis, Normality Test, Frequency Distribution and Multiple Regression Analysis to obtain the hidden patterns with respect to Dimensions of Gold Futures with special reference to Bullion Market for establishing hypotheses and achieving objectives of the research. The Multiple Regression Analysis was employed because the samples were normally distributed and this method helped to find the degree of influencing factors of volatility on dimensions of gold futures.

5.1 LAYOUT OF THE DATA ANALYSIS

Multiple Regression Analysis was employed for data analysis for identifying the degree of influencing factors of volatility on dimensions of gold futures. The Layout of the Statistical Techniques is given bellow:

Table 5.1 contains the common factors influencing the volatility in the bullion market with respect to gold

Various factors were extracted by talking to Stock Market Expert, Investors of Gold Futures, Gold Dealers and Stock Brokers. The commonly observed influencing factors of volatility in the bullion market are "Global Crisis", "Inflation Rate", "Value of the U.S. Dollar", "Interest Rates", "Consumption of Gold", "Recession in world market" "Gold demand and supply" and "REPO Rate".

Table 5.2 shows various dimensions of Gold Futures with special reference to bullion market

Various factors were identified by talking to Export market expert, Investors of Gold Futures, Gold Dealers and Stock Brokers. The commonly observed dimensions of Gold Futures with special reference to bullion market are "Functional Dimension", "Demographic Dimension", "Opportunity Dimension" and "Financial Dimension".

Table 5.3 to Table 5.18 indicates summary of Adjusted Squired Multiple R

The tables contain the summary of Adjusted Squired Multiple R that indicates the degree of influencing factors of volatility on dimensions of gold futures.

Table 5.19 shows the comparison summary of percentage of Adjusted Squared Multiple Regression Analysis with respect to different Category of Respondents

The tables contain the comparison summary of percentage of Adjusted Squared Multiple Regression Analysis with respect to different Category of Respondents.

Table 5.20 contains the common risks in investing gold and need to be addressed in view of the volatility

Various risks in investing gold were extracted by talking to Export market expert, Investors of Gold Futures, Gold Dealers and Stock Brokers. The common risks in investing gold are "Price Risk", "Exchange Rate Risk", "Bankruptcy of Bank", "Trading Interruptions", "Operational Risk", "Identity Theft", "Insurance Exclusions", and "Termination of Gold Republic".

Table 5.21 contains the hedging mechanism to counter various risks associated with volatility

Various hedging mechanism were extracted by talking to Export market expert, Investors of Gold Futures, Gold Dealers and Stock Brokers. The common hedging mechanism to counter various risks associated with volatility are "Stocks", "Exchange-traded funds", "Insurance", "Forward contracts", "Swaps", "Options", "Over-the-counter", and "Futures contracts".

Table 5.22 shows the compare and contrasts the dimensions of commodity futures of bullion market of select Western markets with India

The trends of Gold Futures were identified from the secondary data available in various sources like articles, government websites, company websites etc. The Trends of Gold Futures with reference to Western and India Bullion Market are shown with necessary information.

5.2 DETAILS OF DATA ANALYSIS WITH HYPOTHESIS TESTING

The collected data were analyzed by employing the statistical techniques of Multiple Regression Analysis to obtain the hidden patterns with respect to dimensions of Gold Futures with special reference to bullion market.

5.2.1 Analysis related to the study and understands the volatility in the bullion market with respect to gold

The analysis related to the study and understands the volatility in the bullion market with respect to gold. Various factors were extracted by talking to Stock market expert, Investors of Gold Futures, Gold Dealers and Stock Brokers. Table 5.1 shows the factors influencing the volatility in the bullion market with respect to gold.

"Global Crisis" is the factor that influences the volatility in the bullion market with respect to gold. The experts have given their first preferences around 21 percent of respondents.

"Inflation Rate" is the factor that influences the volatility in the bullion market with respect to gold. The experts have given their first preferences around 18 percent of respondents.

"Value of the U.S. Dollar" is the factor that influences the volatility in the bullion market with respect to gold. The experts have given their first preferences around 15 percent of respondents.

"Interest Rates" is the factor that influences the volatility in the bullion market with respect to gold. The experts have given their first preferences around 13 percent of respondents.

"Consumption of Gold" is the factor that influences the volatility in the bullion market with respect to gold. The experts have given their first preferences around 11 percent of respondents.

"Recession in world market" is the factor that influences the volatility in the bullion market with respect to gold. The experts have given their first preferences around 9 percent of respondents.

"Gold demand and supply" is the factor that influences the volatility in the bullion market with respect to gold. The experts have given their first preferences around 7 percent of respondents.

"REPO Rate" is the factor that influences the volatility in the bullion market with respect to gold. The experts have given their first preferences around 7 percent of respondents.

Based the result from table no 5.1, most of the expert of export market, gold dealers and investors of gold futures indicated the Global Crisis as the major influencing factor in the bullion market with reference to gold. Similarly, the Inflation Rate, Value of the U.S. Dollar and Interest Rates identified close frequency of occurrence in percentage that influence the bullion market with reference to gold.

Table - 5.1
Factors influencing the volatility in bullion market with respect to gold

SL. No.	Factors influencing the volatility in the bullion market	Frequency of Occurrence in Percentage
1	Global Crisis	21
2	Inflation Rate	18
3	Value of the U.S. Dollar	15
4	Interest Rates	13
5	Consumption of Gold	11
6	Recession in world market	9
7	Gold demand and supply	7
8	REPO Rate	6

Source: Compiled By the Researcher

Graph - 5.1

Factors influencing the volatility in bullion market with respect to gold

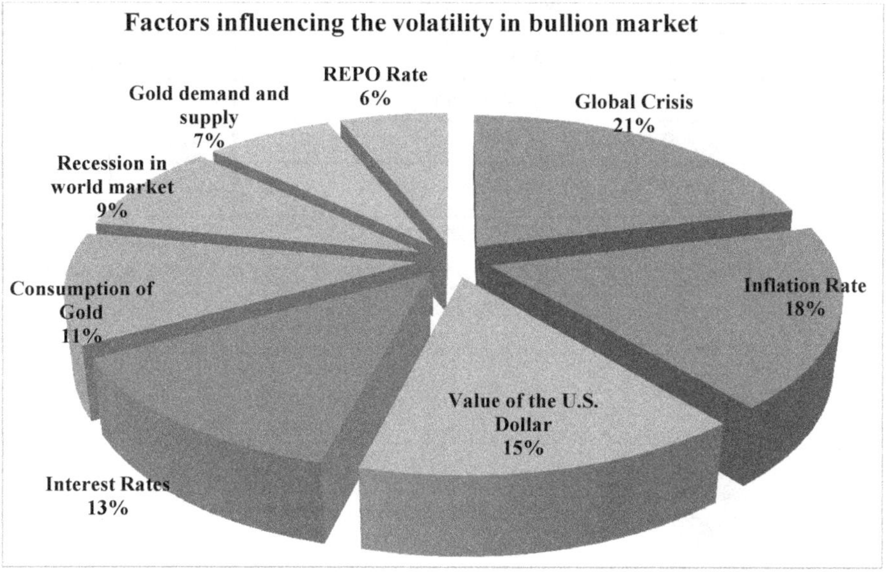

5.2.2 Common dimensions of Gold Futures with special reference to bullion market

The analysis is based on the dimensions of Gold Futures with special reference to bullion market. Various dimensions of Gold Futures with special reference to bullion market have extracted by talking to bullion market practitioners, expert of stock market and gold dealers.

The experts and stock market practitioners have given their valuable opinion and the most frequent opinion occurrence predominantly regarding dimensions of Gold Futures with special reference to bullion market. Table 5.2 shows the dimensions of Gold Futures with special reference to bullion market.

Table - 5.2
The dimensions of Gold Futures with reference to bullion market

SL. No.	Dimensions of Gold Futures	Frequency of Occurrence in Percentage
1	Functional Dimension	31
2	Demographic Dimension	27
3	Opportunity Dimension	22
4	Financial Dimension	20

Source: Compiled By the Researcher

The experts' opinion summarizes the Industrial Usage and Individual Usage of gold that represent the "Functional Dimension" of gold futures. The Frequency of Occurrence in Percentage of Functional Dimension was31 percent with special reference to gold futures.

Graph - 5.2
The dimensions of Gold Futures with reference to bullion market

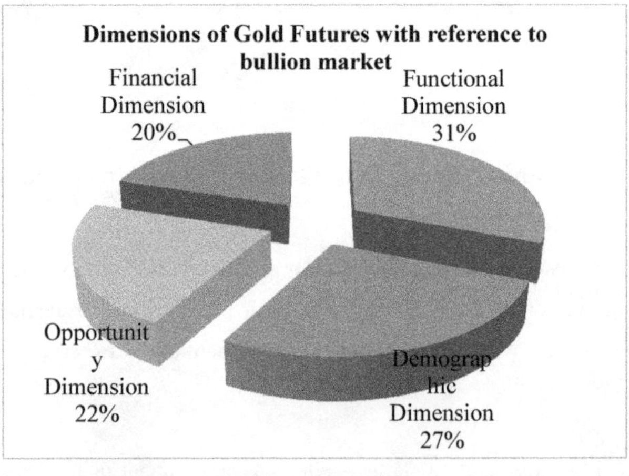

The experts' opinion summarizes the Degree of Savings and Long term investment plan related to gold that represent the "Demographic Dimension" of gold futures. The Frequency of Occurrence in Percentage of Demographic Dimension was27 percent with special reference to gold futures.

The experts' opinion summarizes the Investment during times of economic instability, volatile commodity markets related to gold that represent the "Opportunity Dimension" of gold futures. The Frequency of Occurrence in Percentage of Opportunity Dimension was22 percent with special reference to gold futures.

The experts' opinion summarizes the Resale Value and Loan against the gold related to gold that represent the "Financial Dimension" of gold futures. The Frequency of Occurrence in Percentage of Opportunity Dimension was20 percent with special reference to gold futures.

5.2.3 Analyzing the degree of influencing factors of volatility on dimensions of gold futures

The analysis based on the degree of influencing factors of volatility on dimensions of gold futures. Various factors were extracted by talking to three stakeholders such as Investors of Gold Futures, Gold Dealers and Stock Brokers. In order to get the picture about reality the representations have selected from all the three categories of respondents of 630 samples which were further categorized into 392Investors of Gold Futures, 184Gold Dealers and 4Stock Brokers.

The distributed and collected 630 samples from various categories of respondents and the responses were not same. Since I wanted an authentic proof, so that without any hesitation I can use the t-test and Multiple Regression Analysis, the Normality Test has been employed for the whole sample. There were two Normality Tests have done, one was The Shapiro–Wilk (S-W) - Test and the Kolmogorov–Smirnov (K-S) Test. ANOVA Test (Regression Analysis) was employed to confirm about eight Influencing Factors together influence the Functional Dimension. Similarly, t-test was executed to confirm about individual factors that influence Functional Dimension.

The commonly identifying factors influencing the volatility in the bullion market with respect to gold such as "Global Crisis", "Inflation Rate", "Value of the U.S. Dollar", "Interest Rates", "Consumption of Gold", "Recession in world market", "Gold demand and supply" and "REPO Rate". Various commonly identifying dimensions are: "Functional Dimension", "Demographic Dimension", "Opportunity Dimension" and

"Financial Dimension". The brief result of data analyzing with respect to the degree of influencing factors of volatility on dimensions of gold futures are given bellow:

5.2.3.1 Result of "Functional Dimension" – "Factors influencing the volatility" Multiple Regression Analysis (Investors of Gold Futures)

Multiple Regression Analysis was employed and the summary of the result shown in the Table No. 5.3. "Investors of Gold Futures" were the respondents who have given the valuable impressions regarding factors influencing the volatility.

H_{01}: Eight Factors together do not influence the functional dimension. Or,

Mathematically, ***H_{01}**: [The influence of eight factors on functional dimension] = 0*

The above hypothesis (H_{01}) was tested under two categories namely ANOVA Test (Regression Analysis) and t-test. ANOVA Test (Regression Analysis) was employed to confirm about eight Influencing Factors together influence the Functional Dimension. Similarly, t-test was executed to confirm about individual factors that influence Functional Dimension.

The result of ANOVA (Regression Analysis) test indicates significant at 0.01 level. The result from Table 5.3 indicates, there is high degree of impact of all eight "Influencing Factors" together on "Functional Dimension". So, Null Hypothesis is rejected.

The t-test values of "Inflation Rate", "Value of the U.S. Dollar", "Interest Rates", "Consumption of Gold", "Recession in world market" "Gold demand and supply" and "REPO Rate" are significant at 0.01 level. The results from Table 5.3 related to t-test indicate there is high degree of impact of all the above mentioned "Influencing Factors" individually on "Functional Dimension". So, Null Hypothesis is rejected.

The results from table no 5.3 indicates Adjusted squared multiple R: 0.479, Standard error of estimate: 0.956, the Durbin-Watson D Statistic = 2.387 and First Order Autocorrelation = 0.196and F-ratio is 72.551.

Table – 5.3
Summary of "Functional Dimension" – "Factors influencing the volatility" Multiple Regression Analysis (Investors of Gold Futures)

Highlights of Multiple Regression Analysis

DepVar: Functional Dimension, N: 392, Multiple R: 0.705, Squared multiple R: 0.497, Adjusted squared multiple R: 0.479, Standard error of estimate: 0.956

Summary of Multiple Regression Analysis

Effect	Coeff	Std Error	StdCoeff	Tolerance	t
Constant	-5.302	0.609	0.000	-	-7.065
Global Crisis	-0.055	0.029	-0.116	0.256	-1.829
Inflation Rate	0.327	0.066	0.307	0.271	5.982**
Value of the U.S. Dollar	0.766	0.075	0.739	0.201	10.332**
Interest Rates	0.215	0.060	0.305	0.305	5.225**
Consumption of Gold	0.352	0.055	0.386	0.275	6.315**
Recession in world market	-0.515	0.059	-0.599	0.215	-10.568**
Gold demand and supply	-0.175	0.055	-0.258	0.263	-3.968**
REPO Rate	0.368	0.057	0.298	0.582	6.551**

****Significant at 0.01 level**

Analysis of Variance (ANOVA)

Source	Sum-of-Squares	df	Mean-Square	F-ratio
Regression	530.136	8	66.267	72.551**
Residual	357.625	383	0.915	

****Significant at 0.01 level**

Test for Existence of Correlation Amongst the Error Terms

Durbin-Watson D Statistic = 2.387***; First Order Autocorrelation = 0.196

***Not significant at 0.05 level, where the null hypothesis (Ho) involved was "there is no correlation amongst the residual (error) terms in the regression model". The null hypothesis was not rejected. Thus, absence of correlation and error terms cancelling each other is proved.

Source: Compiled By the Researcher

The summary of results from Table 5.3 related to each causal factor that influences functional Dimension is presented as follows:

As indicated by the ANOVA all the independent variables do influence dependent variable (Functional Dimension). The F-ratio of Functional Dimension and Influencing Factors is 72.551 which is significant at 0.01 level. Therefore, the Regression Model is valid.

Since the Regression Model is valid, the further analysis employed and the degree of influence of all variables put together is 47.9% as indicated by the Adjusted Squired Multiple Regression.

"Value of the U.S. Dollar" actually has the real influence in the dependent variable (Functional Dimension) because the result shows the t-value is 10.332 which is significant at 0.01 level. Remain independent variables can be arranged in the following order as they influence on dependent variable (Functional Dimension) based on the t-value (i) REPO Rate, (ii) Consumption of Gold, (iii) Interest Rates, (iv) Inflation Rate

The independent variable (REPO Rate) actually has the real influence on dependent variable (Functional Dimension) because the result shows the t-value is 6.551 which is significant at 0.01 level.

The independent variable (Consumption of Gold) actually has the real influence on dependent variable (Functional Dimension) because the result shows the t-value is 6.315 which is significant at 0.01 level.

The negative value indicates the negative influence of independent variable towards dependent variable. Following are the two variables that influence negatively: (i) Recession in world market and (ii) Gold demand and supply

The independent variable (Global Crisis) actually don't have any real influence on dependent variable (Functional Dimension) because the result shows the t-value is -1.829 which is not significant at 0.01 level.

5.2.3.2 Result of "Demographic Dimension" – "Factors influencing the volatility" Multiple Regression Analysis (Investors of Gold Futures)

Multiple Regression Analysis was employed and the summary of the result shown in the Table No. 5.4. Investors of Gold Futures were the respondents who have given the valuable impressions regarding influencing factors of volatility on dimensions of gold futures.

H_{02}: Eight Factors together do not influence the demographic dimension.

Or,

Mathematically, H_{02}: *[The influence of eight factors on demographic dimension] = 0*

The above hypothesis (H_{02}) was tested under two categories namely ANOVA Test (Regression Analysis) and t-test. ANOVA Test (Regression Analysis) was employed to confirm about eight Influencing Factors together influence on Demographic Dimension. Similarly, t-test was executed to confirm about individual Influencing Factor that influence on Demographic Dimension.

The result of ANOVA (Regression Analysis) test indicates significant at 0.01 level. The result from Table 5.4 indicates the high degree of impact of all eight factors "Global Crisis", "Inflation Rate", "Value of the U.S. Dollar", "Interest Rates", "Consumption of Gold", "Recession in world market" "Gold demand and supply" and "REPO Rate" together on "Demographic Dimension". So, Null Hypothesis is rejected.

The t-test values of "Consumption of Gold" and "Gold demand and supply" are significant at 0.01 level. The results from Table 5.4 related to t-test indicate there is high degree of impact of "Consumption of Gold" and "Gold demand and supply" individually on "Demographic Dimension". So, Null Hypothesis is rejected.

The results from table no 5.4 indicates Adjusted squared multiple R: 0.215, Standard error of estimate: 1.316, the Durbin-Watson D Statistic = 1.755and First Order Autocorrelation = 0.121and F-ratio is 23.950.

Table – 5.4

Summary of "Demographic Dimension" – "Factors influencing the volatility" Multiple Regression Analysis (Investors of Gold Futures)

Highlights of Multiple Regression Analysis

DepVar: Demographic Dimension, N: 392, Multiple R: 0.473, Squared multiple R: 0.224, Adjuste squared multiple R: 0.215, Standard error of estimate: 1.316

Summary of Multiple Regression Analysis

Effect	Coeff	Std Error	StdCoeff	Tolerance	t
Constant	1.529	0.838	0.000	.	1.705
Global Crisis	-0.053	0.051	-0.087	0.256	-1.065
Inflation Rate	0.116	0.090	0.102	0.271	1.285
Value of the U.S. Dollar	0.025	0.102	0.023	0.201	0.258
Interest Rates	0.059	0.083	0.055	0.305	0.716
Consumption of Gold	0.158	0.075	0.167	0.275	2.115*
Recession in world market	0.000	0.068	0.000	0.215	-0.006
Gold demand and supply	0.336	0.061	0.557	0.263	5.529*
REPO Rate	-0.016	0.079	-0.012	0.582	-0.202

***Significant at 0.05 level, **Significant at 0.01 level**

Analysis of Variance (ANOVA)

Source	Sum-of-Squares	df	Mean-Square	F-ratio
Regression	331.885	8	51.586	23.950**
Residual	677.276	383	1.732	

****Significant at 0.01 level**

Test for Existence of Correlation Amongst the Error Terms

Durbin-Watson D Statistic = 1.755***; First Order Autocorrelation = 0.121

***Not significant at 0.05 level, where the null hypothesis (Ho) involved was "there is no correlatic amongst the residual (error) terms in the regression model". The null hypothesis was not rejecte Thus, absence of correlation and error terms cancelling each other is proved.

Source: Compiled By the Researcher

The summary of results from Table 5.4 related to each causal factor and its influence on demographic Dimension is given bellow:

As indicated by the ANOVA all the independent variables do influence dependent variable (Demographic Dimension). The F-ratio of Demographic Dimension and Influencing Factors is 23.950 which is significant at 0.01 level. Therefore, the Regression Model is valid.

The influence of the error terms as indicated by this is negligible. The null hypothesis involved there is no correlation among the residual error terms in the regression model. The error terms i.e., positive error cancels negative error.

Both of these together indicate the regression model is valid. Since the Regression Model is valid, the further analysis employed and the degree of influence of all variables put together is 21.5% as indicated by the Adjusted Squired Multiple Regression.

Gold demand and supply actually has the real influence on dependent variable (Demographic Dimension), because the result shows the t-value is 5.529 which is significant at 0.01 level.

Similarly, the independent variable (Consumption of Gold) also has the real influence on dependent variable (Demographic Dimension) because the result shows the t-value is 2.115 which is significant at 0.01 level.

The independent variables "Global Crisis", "Inflation Rate", "Value of the U.S. Dollar", "Interest Rates", "Recession in world market" and "REPO Rate" actually don't have real influence on dependent variable (Demographic Dimension) because the result shows the t-values are not significant at 0.01 level.

5.2.3.3 Result of "Opportunity Dimension" – "Factors influencing the volatility" Multiple Regression Analysis (Investors of Gold Futures)

Multiple Regression Analysis was employed and the summary of the result shown in the Table No. 5.5. Investors of Gold Futures were the respondents who have given the valuable impressions regarding influencing factors of volatility on dimensions of gold futures.

H_{03}: Eight Factors together do not influence the opportunity dimension.

Or,

Mathematically, H_{03}: *[The influence of eight factors on opportunity dimension] = 0*

The above hypothesis (H_{03}) was tested under two categories namely ANOVA Test (Regression Analysis) and t-test. ANOVA Test (Regression Analysis) was employed to confirm about eight Influencing Factors together influence on Opportunity Dimension. Similarly, t-test was executed to confirm about all influencing factors individually influence on Opportunity Dimension.

The result of ANOVA (Regression Analysis) test indicates significant at 0.01 level. The result from Table 5.5 indicates there is high degree of impact of all eight "Influencing Factors" together influence on Opportunity Dimension. So, Null Hypothesis is rejected.

The t-test values of "Inflation Rate", "Value of the U.S. Dollar", "Consumption of Gold", "Recession in world market" "Gold demand and supply" and "REPO Rate" are significant at 0.01 level. The results from Table 5.5 related to t-test indicate there is high degree of impact of "Inflation Rate", "Value of the U.S. Dollar", "Consumption of Gold", "Recession in world market" "Gold demand and supply" and "REPO Rate" on "Opportunity Dimension". So, Null Hypothesis is rejected.

The results from table no 5.5 indicates Adjusted squared multiple R: 0.265, Standard error of estimate: 1.319, the Durbin-Watson D Statistic = 1.928 and First Order Autocorrelation = 0.035 and F-ratio is 18.923.

Table – 5.5
Summary of "Opportunity Dimension" – "Factors influencing the volatility" Multiple Regression Analysis (Investors of Gold Futures)

Highlights of Multiple Regression Analysis

DepVar: Opportunity Dimension, N: 392, Multiple R: 0.528, Squared multiple R: 0.279, Adjusted squared multiple R: 0.265 Standard error of estimate: 1.319

Summary of Multiple Regression Analysis

Effect	Coeff	Std Error	StdCoeff	Tolerance	t
Constant	2.336	0.850	0.000	.	2.781
Global Crisis	-0.055	0.051	-0.113	0.256	-1.330
Inflation Rate	0.250	0.090	0.228	0.271	2.768**
Value of the U.S. Dollar	0.225	0.102	0.210	0.201	2.195*
Interest Rates	0.159	0.083	0.150	0.305	1.923
Consumption of Gold	0.536	0.075	0.577	0.275	5.825**
Recession in world market	-0.208	0.068	-0.235	0.215	-3.066**
Gold demand and supply	-0.165	0.061	-0.226	0.263	-2.697**
REPO Rate	-0.252	0.079	-0.198	0.582	-3.199**

***Significant at 0.05 level, **Significant at 0.01 level**

Analysis of Variance (ANOVA)

Source	Sum-of-Squares	df	Mean-Square	F-ratio
Regression	263.577	8	32.935	18.923**
Residual	680.521	383	1.750	

****Significant at 0.01 level**

Test for Existence of Correlation Amongst the Error Terms

Durbin-Watson D Statistic = 1.928***; First Order Autocorrelation = 0.035

***Not significant at 0.05 level, where the null hypothesis (Ho) involved was "there is no correlation amongst the residual (error) terms in the regression model". The null hypothesis was not rejected. Thus, absence of correlation and error terms cancelling each other is proved.

Source: Compiled By the Researcher

The summary of results from Table 5.5 related to each causal factor and its influence on Opportunity Dimensions is given bellow:

As indicated by the ANOVA all the independent variables do influence dependent variable (Opportunity Dimension). The F-ratio of Opportunity Effect and Influencing Factors is 18.923 which is significant at 0.01 level. Therefore, the Regression Model is valid.

Since the Regression Model is valid, the further analysis employed and the degree of influence of all variables put together is 26.5% as indicated by the Adjusted Squired Multiple Regression.

Consumption of Gold actually has the real influence in the dependent variable (Opportunity Dimension). Remain independent variables can be arranged in the following order as they influence on dependent variable (Opportunity Dimension) based on the t-value (i) Inflation Rate and (ii) Value of the U.S. Dollar

The independent variable (Inflation Rate) actually has the real influence on dependent variable (Opportunity Dimension) because the result shows the t-value is 2.768 which is significant at 0.01 level.

The independent variable (Value of the U.S. Dollar) has any real influence on dependent variable (Opportunity effect) because the result shows the t-value is 2.195 which is significant at 0.05 level.

The negative value indicates the negative influence towards dependent variables. Following are the two variables that influence negatively (i) Recession in world market, (ii) Gold demand and supply, (iii) REPO Rate

The independent variable (Global Crisis) actually don't have any real influence on dependent variable (Opportunity Dimension) because the result shows t-value is -1.330 which is not significant at 0.01 level.

5.2.3.4 Result of "Financial Dimension" – "Factors influencing the volatility" Multiple Regression Analysis (Investors of Gold Futures)

Multiple Regression Analysis was employed and the summary of the result shown in the Table No. 5.6. Investors of Gold Futures were the respondents who have given the valuable impressions regarding influencing factors of volatility on dimensions of gold futures.

H_{04}: The Eight Factors together do not influence the financial dimension.

Or,

Mathematically, H_{04}: *[The influence of eight factors on financial dimension] = 0*

The above hypothesis (H_{04}) was tested under two categories namely ANOVA Test (Regression Analysis) and t-test. ANOVA Test (Regression Analysis) was employed to confirm about eight Influencing Factors together influence on Financial Dimension. Similarly, t-test was executed to confirm about all influencing factors individually influence on Financial Dimension.

The result of ANOVA (Regression Analysis) test indicates significant at 0.01 level. The result from Table 5.6 indicates there is high degree of impact of all eight "Influencing Factors" together influence on Financial Dimension. So, Null Hypothesis is rejected.

The t-test values of "Inflation Rate", "Value of the U.S. Dollar", "Consumption of Gold", "Gold demand and supply" and "REPO Rate" are significant at 0.01 level.
The results from Table 5.6 related to t-test indicate there is high degree of impact of "Inflation Rate", "Value of the U.S. Dollar", "Consumption of Gold", "Gold demand and supply" and "REPO Rate" on "Financial Dimension". So, Null Hypothesis is rejected.

The results from table no 5.6 indicates Adjusted squared multiple R: 0.372, Standard error of estimate: 1.317, the Durbin-Watson D Statistic = 1.868 and First Order Autocorrelation = 0.069 and F-ratio is 30.585.

Table – 5.6
Summary of "Financial Dimension" – "Factors influencing the volatility" Multiple Regression Analysis (Investors of Gold Futures)

Highlights of Multiple Regression Analysis

DepVar: Financial Dimension, N: 392, Multiple R: 0.620, Squared multiple R: 0.385, Adjusted squared multiple R: 0.372, Standard error of estimate: 1.317

Summary of Multiple Regression Analysis

Effect	Coeff	Std Error	StdCoeff	Tolerance	t
Constant	-1.175	0.839	0.000	.	-1.500
Global Crisis	0.031	0.051	0.059	0.256	0.755
Inflation Rate	0.538	0.090	0.370	0.271	5.855**
Value of the U.S. Dollar	0.351	0.102	0.305	0.201	3.551**
Interest Rates	0.035	0.083	0.030	0.305	0.510
Consumption of Gold	0.162	0.075	0.165	0.275	2.169*
Recession in world market	-0.025	0.068	-0.026	0.215	-0.367
Gold demand and supply	-0.123	0.061	-0.156	0.263	-2.021*
REPO Rate	-0.205	0.079	-0.158	0.582	-2.598*

***Significant at 0.05 level, **Significant at 0.01 level**

Analysis of Variance (ANOVA)

Source	Sum-of-Squares	df	Mean-Square	F-ratio
Regression	525.712	8	53.089	30.585**
Residual	678.685	383	1.736	

****Significant at 0.01 level**

Test for Existence of Correlation Amongst the Error Terms

Durbin-Watson D Statistic = 1.868***; First Order Autocorrelation = 0.069

***Not significant at 0.05 level, where the null hypothesis (Ho) involved was "there is no correlation amongst the residual (error) terms in the regression model". The null hypothesis was not rejected. Thus, absence of correlation and error terms cancelling each other is proved.

Source: Compiled By the Researcher

The summary of results from Table 5.6 related to each causal factor and its influence on Financial Dimension is presented as follows:

As indicated by the ANOVA all the independent variables do influence dependent variable (Financial Dimension). The F-ratio of Financial Dimension and Influencing Factors is 30.585 which are significant at 0.01 level. Therefore, the Regression Model is valid.

Since the Regression Model is valid, the further analysis employed and the degree of influence of all variables put together is 37.2% as indicated by the Adjusted Squired Multiple Regression.

Inflation Rate actually has the real influence on dependent variable (Financial Dimension). Remain independent variables can be arranged in the following order as they influence on dependent variable (Financial Dimension) based on the t-value: (i) Value of the U.S. Dollar and (ii) Consumption of Gold.

The independent variable (Value of the U.S. Dollar) actually has the real influence on dependent variable (Financial Dimension) because the result shows the t-value is 3.551 which is highly significant at 0.01 level. Similarly, the independent variable (Consumption of Gold) actually has the real influence on dependent variable (Financial Dimension) because the result shows the t-value is 2.169 which is significant at 0.05 level.

The independent variable (Global Crisis) actually don't have any real influence on dependent variable (Financial Dimension) because the result shows un-standardized Coefficient is 0.031 and standardized coefficient is 0.059 which are weak uphill (positive) linear relationship and the t-value is 0.755 which is not significant at 0.01 level.

Similarly, the independent variable (Interest Rates) actually don't have any real influence on dependent variable (Financial Dimension) because the result shows un-standardized Coefficient is 0.035 and standardized coefficient is 0.030 which are weak uphill (positive) linear relationship and the t-value is 0.510 which is not significant at 0.01 level.

5.2.3.5 Result of "Functional Dimension" – "Factors influencing the volatility" Multiple Regression Analysis (Gold Dealers)

Multiple Regression Analysis was employed and the summary of the result shown in the Table No. 5.7. Gold dealers were the respondents who have given the valuable impressions regarding factors influencing the volatility.

H_{01}: Eight Factors together do not influence the functional dimension.

Or,

Mathematically, $\boldsymbol{H_{01}}$: *[The influence of eight factors on functional dimension] = 0*

The above hypothesis (H_{01}) was tested under two categories namely ANOVA Test (Regression Analysis) and t-test. ANOVA Test (Regression Analysis) was employed to confirm about eight Influencing Factors together influence the Functional Dimension. Similarly, t-test was executed to confirm about individual factors that influence Functional Dimension.

The result of ANOVA (Regression Analysis) test indicates significant at 0.01 level. The result from Table 5.7 indicates, there is high degree of impact of all eight "Influencing Factors" together on "Functional Dimension". So, Null Hypothesis is rejected.

The t-test values of "Inflation Rate", "Value of the U.S. Dollar", "Interest Rates", "Consumption of Gold", "Recession in world market" "Gold demand and supply" and "REPO Rate" are significant at 0.01 level.

The results from Table 5.7 related to t-test indicate there is high degree of impact of all the above mentioned "Influencing Factors" individually on "Functional Dimension". So, Null Hypothesis is rejected.

The results from table no 5.7 indicates Adjusted squared multiple R: 0.005, Standard error of estimate: 0.627, the Durbin-Watson D Statistic = 1.387and First Order Autocorrelation = 0.558 and F-ratio is 1.398.

Table – 5.7
Summary of "Functional Dimension" – "Factors influencing the volatility" Multiple Regression Analysis (Gold Dealers)

Highlights of Multiple Regression Analysis

DepVar: Functional Dimension, N: 184, Multiple R: 0.155, Squared multiple R: 0.025, Adjusted squared multiple R: 0.005, Standard error of estimate: 0.627

Summary of Multiple Regression Analysis

Effect	Coeff	Std Error	StdCoeff	Tolerance	t
Constant	-5.302	0.609	0.000	.	-5.065
Global Crisis	-0.055	0.029	0.036	0.056	-1.019
Inflation Rate	0.027	0.066	0.017	0.071	1.082
Value of the U.S. Dollar	0.066	0.075	0.039	0.101	1.032
Interest Rates	0.085	0.060	0.065	0.095	1.120
Consumption of Gold	0.105	0.055	0.098	0.075	0.215
Recession in world market	-0.115	0.059	-0.079	0.015	0.568
Gold demand and supply	-0.075	0.055	-0.058	0.063	1.008
REPO Rate	0.118	0.057	0.108	0.082	0.551

***Significant at 0.05 level, **Significant at 0.01 level**

Analysis of Variance (ANOVA)

Source	Sum-of-Squares	df	Mean-Square	F-ratio
Regression	239.136	4	29.882	1.398
Residual	357.625	179	21.375	

****Significant at 0.01 level**

Test for Existence of Correlation Amongst the Error Terms

Durbin-Watson D Statistic = 1.387***; First Order Autocorrelation = 0.558

***Not significant at 0.05 level, where the null hypothesis (Ho) involved was "there is no correlation amongst the residual (error) terms in the regression model". The null hypothesis was not rejected. Thus, absence of correlation and error terms cancelling each other is proved.

Source: Compiled By the Researcher

5.2.3.6 Result of "Demographic Dimension" – "Factors influencing the volatility" Multiple Regression Analysis (Gold Dealers)

Multiple Regression Analysis was employed and the summary of the result shown in the Table No. 5.8. Gold dealers were the respondents who have given the valuable impressions regarding influencing factors of volatility on dimensions of gold futures.

H_{02}: Eight Factors together do not influence the demographic dimension.

Or,

Mathematically, H_{02}: *[The influence of eight factors on demographic dimension] = 0*

The above hypothesis (H_{02}) was tested under two categories namely ANOVA Test (Regression Analysis) and t-test. ANOVA Test (Regression Analysis) was employed to confirm about eight Influencing Factors together influence on Demographic Dimension. Similarly, t-test was executed to confirm about individual Influencing Factor that influence on Demographic Dimension.

The result of ANOVA (Regression Analysis) test indicates significant at 0.01 level. The result from Table 5.8 indicates the high degree of impact of all eight factors "Global Crisis", "Inflation Rate", "Value of the U.S. Dollar", "Interest Rates", "Consumption of Gold", "Recession in world market" "Gold demand and supply" and "REPO Rate" together on "Demographic Dimension". So, Null Hypothesis is rejected.

The t-test values of "Consumption of Gold" and "Gold demand and supply" are significant at 0.01 level. The results from Table 5.8 related to t-test indicate there is high degree of impact of "Consumption of Gold" and "Gold demand and supply" individually on "Demographic Dimension". So, Null Hypothesis is rejected.

The results from table no 5.8 indicates Adjusted squared multiple R: 0.107, Standard error of estimate: 0.902, the Durbin-Watson D Statistic = 1.686and First Order Autocorrelation = 0.155and F-ratio is 6.982.

Table – 5.8
Summary of "Demographic Dimension" – "Factors influencing the volatility" Multiple Regression Analysis (Gold Dealers)

Highlights of Multiple Regression Analysis

DepVar: Demographic Dimension, N: 184, Multiple R: 0.355, Squared multiple R: 0.125, Adjusted squared multiple R: 0.107, Standard error of estimate: 0.902

Summary of Multiple Regression Analysis

Effect	Coeff	Std Error	StdCoeff	Tolerance	t
Constant	3.208	3.507	0.000	.	0.951
Global Crisis	0.107	0.727	0.219	0.002	0.157
Inflation Rate	0.075	0.202	0.191	0.017	0.372
Value of the U.S. Dollar	-0.129	3.205	-0.055	0.002	-0.050
Interest Rates	.0.125	2.108.	.0.068	.0.155	0.056.
Consumption of Gold	0.028	0.801	-0.011	0.025	-0.032
Recession in world market	0.058	0.630	-0.027	0.055	-0.052
Gold demand and supply	-0.018	0.831	-0.009	0.025	-0.022
REPO Rate	0.068	0.502	-0.071	0.075	-0.062

***Significant at 0.05 level, **Significant at 0.01 level**

Analysis of Variance (ANOVA)

Source	Sum-of-Squares	df	Mean-Square	F-ratio
Regression	22.709	4	5.677	6.982**
Residual	158.571	179	0.813	

****Significant at 0.01 level**

Test for Existence of Correlation Amongst the Error Terms

Durbin-Watson D Statistic = 1.686***; First Order Autocorrelation = 0.155

***Not significant at 0.05 level, where the null hypothesis (Ho) involved was "there is no correlation amongst the residual (error) terms in the regression model". The null hypothesis was not rejected. Thus, absence of correlation and error terms cancelling each other proved.

Source: Compiled By the Researcher

5.2.3.7 Result of "Opportunity Dimension" – "Factors influencing the volatility" Multiple Regression Analysis (Gold Dealers)

Multiple Regression Analysis was employed and the summary of the result shown in the Table No. 5.9. Gold dealers were the respondents who have given the valuable impressions regarding influencing factors of volatility on dimensions of gold futures.

H_{03}: Eight Factors together do not influence the opportunity dimension.

Or,

Mathematically, $\boldsymbol{H_{03}}$: *[The influence of eight factors on opportunity dimension] = 0*

The above hypothesis (H_{03}) was tested under two categories namely ANOVA Test (Regression Analysis) and t-test. ANOVA Test (Regression Analysis) was employed to confirm about eight Influencing Factors together influence on Opportunity Dimension. Similarly, t-test was executed to confirm about all influencing factors individually influence on Opportunity Dimension.

The result of ANOVA (Regression Analysis) test indicates significant at 0.01 level. The result from Table 5.9 indicates there is high degree of impact of all eight "Influencing Factors" together influence on Opportunity Dimension. So, Null Hypothesis is rejected.

The t-test values of "Inflation Rate", "Value of the U.S. Dollar", "Consumption of Gold", "Recession in world market" "Gold demand and supply" and "REPO Rate" are significant at 0.01 level. The results from Table 5.9 related to t-test indicate there is high degree of impact of "Inflation Rate", "Value of the U.S. Dollar", "Consumption of Gold", "Recession in world market" "Gold demand and supply" and "REPO Rate" on "Opportunity Dimension". So, Null Hypothesis is rejected.

The results from table no 5.9 indicates Adjusted squared multiple R: 0.176, Standard error of estimate: 0.726, the Durbin-Watson D Statistic = 1.108and First Order Autocorrelation = 0.155 and F-ratio is 11.620.

Table – 5.9

Summary of "Opportunity Dimension" – "Factors influencing the volatility" Multiple Regression Analysis (Gold Dealers)

Highlights of Multiple Regression Analysis

DepVar: Opportunity Dimension, N: 184, Multiple R: 0.539, Squared multiple R: 0.192
Adjusted squared multiple R: 0.176 Standard error of estimate: 0.726

Summary of Multiple Regression Analysis

Effect	Coeff	Std Error	StdCoeff	Tolerance	t
Constant	21.711	2.955	0.000	.	7.357
Global Crisis	.0.032	.0.235	.0.022	.0.087	.0.678
Inflation Rate	-0.319	0.081	-0.972	0.069	-3.958**
Value of the U.S. Dollar	.0.039	.0.335	.0.027	.0.067	.0.558
Interest Rates	-1.315	0.228	-1.617	0.053	-5.780**
Consumption of Gold	.0.055	.0.201	.0.028	.0.091	.0.750
Recession in world market	-0.535	0.107	-0.788	0.166	-5.985**
Gold demand and supply	.0.098	.0.135	.0.082	.0.055	.0.530
REPO Rate	0.025	0.115	0.025	0.325	0.215

****Significant at 0.01 level**

Analysis of Variance (ANOVA)

Source	Sum-of-Squares	df	Mean-Square	F-ratio
Regression	25.579	4	6.120	11.620**
Residual	102.701	179	0.527	

****Significant at 0.01 level**

Test for Existence of Correlation Amongst the Error Terms

Durbin-Watson D Statistic = 1.108***; First Order Autocorrelation = 0.552

***Not significant at 0.05 level, where the null hypothesis (Ho) involved was "there is no correlation amongst the residual (error) terms in the regression model". The null hypothesis was not rejected. Thus, absence of correlation and error terms cancelling each other is proved.

Source: Compiled By the Researcher

5.2.3.8 Result of "Financial Dimension" – "Factors influencing the volatility" Multiple Regression Analysis (Gold Dealers)

Multiple Regression Analysis was employed and the summary of the result shown in the Table No. 5.10. Gold dealers were the respondents who have given the valuable impressions regarding influencing factors of volatility on dimensions of gold futures.

H_{04}: The Eight Factors together do not influence the financial dimension.

Or,

Mathematically, ***H_{04}****: [The influence of eight factors on financial dimension] = 0*

The above hypothesis (H_{04}) was tested under two categories namely ANOVA Test (Regression Analysis) and t-test. ANOVA Test (Regression Analysis) was employed to confirm about eight Influencing Factors together influence onFinancial Dimension. Similarly, t-test was executed to confirm about all influencingfactors individually influence on Financial Dimension.

The result of ANOVA (Regression Analysis) test indicates significant at 0.01 level. The result from Table 5.10 indicates there is high degree of impact of all eight "Influencing Factors" together influence on Financial Dimension. So, Null Hypothesis is rejected.

The t-test values of "Inflation Rate", "Value of the U.S. Dollar", "Consumption of Gold", "Gold demand and supply" and "REPO Rate" are significant at 0.01 level. The results from Table 5.10 related to t-test indicate there is high degree of impact of "Inflation Rate", "Value of the U.S. Dollar", "Consumption of Gold", "Gold demand and supply" and "REPO Rate" on "Financial Dimension". So, Null Hypothesis is rejected.

The results from table no 5.10 indicates Adjusted squared multiple R: 0.222, Standard error of estimate: 0.802, the Durbin-Watson D Statistic = 1.762and First Order Autocorrelation = 0.112 and F-ratio is 15.237.

Table – 5.10
Summary of "Financial Dimension" – "Factors influencing the volatility" Multiple Regression Analysis (Gold Dealers)

Highlights of Multiple Regression Analysis

DepVar: Financial Dimension, N: 184, Multiple R: 0.588, Squared multiple R: 0.238, Adjusted squared multiple R: 0.222, Standard error of estimate: 0.802

Summary of Multiple Regression Analysis

Effect	Coeff	Std Error	StdCoeff	Tolerance	t
Constant	12.193	2.257	0.000	.	5.526
Global Crisis	0.652	0.236	1.505	0.015	2.756**
Inflation Rate	.0.120	0.312.	.0.098	.0.121	.1.023
Value of the U.S. Dollar	-5.819	1.599	-2.155	0.079	-3.215**
Interest Rates	0.112.	0.387.	0.087.	.0.082	0.065.
Consumption of Gold	0.155	0.322.	0.098.	.0.110	0.678.
Recession in world market	-0.500	0.090	-0.518	0.289	-5.559**
Gold demand and supply	2.176	0.530	1.172	0.058	5.106**
REPO Rate	0.119	0.355.	0.082	.0.220	0.578.

Significant at 0.01 level

Analysis of Variance (ANOVA)

Source	Sum-of-Squares	df	Mean-Square	F-ratio
Regression	39.232	4	9.808	15.237**
Residual	125.523	179	0.655	

Significant at 0.01 level

Test for Existence of Correlation Amongst the Error Terms

Durbin-Watson D Statistic = 1.762***; First Order Autocorrelation = 0.112

***Not significant at 0.05 level, where the null hypothesis (Ho) involved was "there is no correlation amongst the residual (error) terms in the regression model". The null hypothesis was not rejected. Thus, absence of correlation and error terms cancelling each other is proved.

Source: Compiled By the Researcher

5.2.3.9 Result of "Functional Dimension" – "Factors influencing the volatility" Multiple Regression Analysis (Stock Brokers)

Multiple Regression Analysis was employed and the summary of the result shown in the Table No. 5.11. Stock Brokers were the respondents who have given the valuable impressions regarding factors influencing the volatility.

H_{01}: Eight Factors together do not influence the functional dimension.

Or,

Mathematically, ***H_{01}****: [The influence of eight factors on functional dimension] = 0*

The above hypothesis (H_{01}) was tested under two categories namely ANOVA Test (Regression Analysis) and t-test. ANOVA Test (Regression Analysis) was employed to confirm about eight Influencing Factors together influence the Functional Dimension. Similarly, t-test was executed to confirm about individual factors that influence Functional Dimension.

The result of ANOVA (Regression Analysis) test indicates significant at 0.01 level. The result from Table 5.11 indicates, there is high degree of impact of all eight "Influencing Factors" together on "Functional Dimension". So, Null Hypothesis is rejected.

The t-test values of "Inflation Rate", "Value of the U.S. Dollar", "Interest Rates", "Consumption of Gold", "Recession in world market" "Gold demand and supply" and "REPO Rate" are significant at 0.01 level. The results from Table 5.11 related to t-test indicate there is high degree of impact of all the above mentioned "Influencing Factors" individually on "Functional Dimension". So, Null Hypothesis is rejected.

The results from table no 5.11 indicates Adjusted squared multiple R: 0.559, Standard error of estimate: 0.802, the Durbin-Watson D Statistic = 1.762and First Order Autocorrelation = 0.112 and F-ratio is 32.583.

Table – 5.11

Summary of "Functional Dimension" – "Factors influencing the volatility" Multiple Regression Analysis (Stock Brokers)

Highlights of Multiple Regression Analysis

DepVar: Functional Dimension, N: 54, Multiple R: 0.760, Squared multiple R: 0.577, Adjusted squared multiple R: 0.559, Standard error of estimate: 0.721

Summary of Multiple Regression Analysis

Effect	Coeff	Std Error	StdCoeff	Tolerance	t
Constant	6.035	1.291	0.000	.	6.035
Global Crisis	-0.133	0.055	-0.250	0.356	-0.133
Inflation Rate	0.062	0.061	0.063	0.591	0.062
Value of the U.S. Dollar	0.508	0.088	0.506	0.286	0.508
Interest Rates	0.129	0.075	0.165	0.252	0.129
Consumption of Gold	-0.019	0.073	-0.018	0.553	-0.019
Recession in world market	-0.327	0.056	-0.506	0.682	-0.327
Gold demand and supply	-0.556	0.062	-0.523	0.653	-0.556
REPO Rate	0.561	0.065	0.587	0.693	0.561

***Significant at 0.05 level, **Significant at 0.01 level**

Analysis of Variance (ANOVA)

Source	Sum-of-Squares	df	Mean-Square	F-ratio
Regression	135.505	4	16.938	32.583**
Residual	99.290	49	0.520	

****Significant at 0.01 level**

Test for Existence of Correlation Amongst the Error Terms

Durbin-Watson D Statistic = 2.101***; First Order Autocorrelation = 0.062

***Not significant at 0.05 level, where the null hypothesis (Ho) involved was "there is no correlation amongst the residual (error) terms in the regression model". The null hypothesis was not rejected. Thus, absence of correlation and error terms cancelling each other is proved.

Source: Compiled By the Researcher

5.2.3.10 Result of "Demographic Dimension" – "Factors influencing the volatility" Multiple Regression Analysis (Stock Brokers)

Multiple Regression Analysis was employed and the summary of the result shown in the Table No. 5.12. Stock Brokers were the respondents who have given the valuable impressions regarding influencing factors of volatility on dimensions of gold futures.

H_{02}: Eight Factors together do not influence the demographic dimension.

Or,

Mathematically, $\boldsymbol{H_{02}}$: *[The influence of eight factors on demographic dimension] = 0*

The above hypothesis (H_{02}) was tested under two categories namely ANOVA Test (Regression Analysis) and t-test. ANOVA Test (Regression Analysis) was employed to confirm about eight Influencing Factors together influence on Demographic Dimension. Similarly, t-test was executed to confirm about individual Influencing Factor that influence on Demographic Dimension.

The result of ANOVA (Regression Analysis) test indicates significant at 0.01 level. The result from Table 5.12 indicates the high degree of impact of all eight factors "Global Crisis", "Inflation Rate", "Value of the U.S. Dollar", "Interest Rates", "Consumption of Gold", "Recession in world market" "Gold demand and supply" and "REPO Rate" together on "Demographic Dimension". So, Null Hypothesis is rejected.

The t-test values of "Consumption of Gold" and "Gold demand and supply" are significant at 0.01 level. The results from Table 5.12related to t-test indicate there is high degree of impact of "Consumption of Gold" and "Gold demand and supply" individually on "Demographic Dimension". So, Null Hypothesis is rejected.

Table – 5.12

Summary of "Demographic Dimension" – "Factors influencing the volatility" Multiple Regression Analysis (Stock Brokers)

Highlights of Multiple Regression Analysis

DepVar: Demographic Dimension, N: 54, Multiple R: 0.299 Squared multiple R: 0.089, Adjusted squared multiple R: 0.051, Standard error of estimate: 1.052

Summary of Multiple Regression Analysis

Effect	Coeff	Std Error	StdCoeff	Tolerance	t
Constant	5.035	1.883	0.000	.	5.035
Global Crisis	-0.150	0.065	-0.255	0.356	-0.150
Inflation Rate	-0.001	0.088	-0.001	0.591	-0.001
Value of the U.S. Dollar	-0.012	0.129	-0.012	0.286	-0.012
Interest Rates	0.185	0.109	0.236	0.252	0.185
Consumption of Gold	0.315	0.107	0.305	0.553	0.315
Recession in world market	-0.035	0.067	-0.053	0.682	-0.035
Gold demand and supply	0.156	0.090	0.150	0.653	0.156
REPO Rate	-0.020	0.095	-0.018	0.693	-0.020

***Significant at 0.05 level, **Significant at 0.01 level**

Analysis of Variance (ANOVA)

Source	Sum-of-Squares	df	Mean-Square	F-ratio
Regression	50.707	4	5.088	5.600**
Residual	211.213	49	1.106	

****Significant at 0.01 level**

Test for Existence of Correlation Amongst the Error Terms

Durbin-Watson D Statistic = 1.698***; First Order Autocorrelation = 0.155

***Not significant at 0.05 level, where the null hypothesis (Ho) involved was "there is no correlation amongst the residual (error) terms in the regression model". The null hypothesis was not rejected. Thus, absence of correlation and error terms cancelling each other is proved.

Source: Compiled By the Researcher

5.2.3.11 Result of "Opportunity Dimension" – "Factors influencing the volatility" Multiple Regression Analysis (Stock Brokers)

Multiple Regression Analysis was employed and the summary of the result shown in the Table No. 5.13. Stock Brokers were the respondents who have given the valuable impressions regarding influencing factors of volatility on dimensions of gold futures.

H_{03}: Eight Factors together do not influence the opportunity dimension.

Or,

Mathematically, H_{03}: *[The influence of eight factors on opportunity dimension] = 0*

The above hypothesis (H_{03}) was tested under two categories namely ANOVA Test (Regression Analysis) and t-test. ANOVA Test (Regression Analysis) was employed to confirm about eight Influencing Factors together influence on Opportunity Dimension. Similarly, t-test was executed to confirm about all influencing factors individually influence on Opportunity Dimension.

The result of ANOVA (Regression Analysis) test indicates significant at 0.01 level. The result from Table 5.13 indicates there is high degree of impact of all eight "Influencing Factors" together influence on Opportunity Dimension. So, Null Hypothesis is rejected.

The t-test values of "Inflation Rate", "Value of the U.S. Dollar", "Consumption of Gold", "Recession in world market" "Gold demand and supply" and "REPO Rate" are significant at 0.01 level. The results from Table 5.13 related to t-test indicate there is high degree of impact of "Inflation Rate", "Value of the U.S. Dollar", "Consumption of Gold", "Recession in world market" "Gold demand and supply" and "REPO Rate" on "Opportunity Dimension". So, Null Hypothesis is rejected.

Table – 5.13
Summary of "Opportunity Dimension" – "Factors influencing the volatility" Multiple Regression Analysis (Stock Brokers)

Highlights of Multiple Regression Analysis

DepVar: Opportunity Dimension, N: 54, Multiple R: 0.555, Squared multiple R: 0.307, Adjusted squared multiple R: 0.278 Standard error of estimate: 0.860

Summary of Multiple Regression Analysis

Effect	Coeff	Std Error	StdCoeff	Tolerance	t
Constant	5.967	1.550	0.000	.	3.226
Global Crisis	0.012	0.052	0.025	0.356	0.239
Inflation Rate	0.291	0.072	0.315	0.591	5.022**
Value of the U.S. Dollar	-0.118	0.105	-0.126	0.286	-1.115
Interest Rates	-0.020	0.089	-0.027	0.252	-0.218
Consumption of Gold	0.078	0.087	0.081	0.553	0.895
Recession in world market	-0.075	0.055	-0.100	0.682	-1.367
Gold demand and supply	-0.377	0.075	-0.383	0.653	-5.102**
REPO Rate	0.052	0.078	0.039	0.693	0.553

**Significant at 0.01 level

Analysis of Variance (ANOVA)

Source	Sum-of-Squares	df	Mean-Square	F-ratio
Regression	62.695	4	7.837	10.595**
Residual	151.286	49	0.750	

**Significant at 0.01 level

Test for Existence of Correlation Amongst the Error Terms

Durbin-Watson D Statistic = 1.950***; First Order Autocorrelation = 0.021

***Not significant at 0.05 level, where the null hypothesis (Ho) involved was "there is no correlation amongst the residual (error) terms in the regression model". The null hypothesis was not rejected. Thus, absence of correlation and error terms cancelling each other is proved.

Source: Compiled By the Researcher

5.2.3.12 Result of "Financial Dimension" – "Factors influencing the volatility" Multiple Regression Analysis (Stock Brokers)

Multiple Regression Analysis was employed and the summary of the result shown in the Table No. 5.14. Stock Brokers were the respondents who have given the valuable impressions regarding influencing factors of volatility on dimensions of gold futures.

H_{04}: The Eight Factors together do not influence the financial dimension.

Or,

Mathematically, H_{04}: *[The influence of eight factors on financial dimension] = 0*

The above hypothesis (H_{04}) was tested under two categories namely ANOVA Test (Regression Analysis) and t-test. ANOVA Test (Regression Analysis) was employed to confirm about eight Influencing Factors together influence on Financial Dimension. Similarly, t-test was executed to confirm about all influencing factors individually influence on Financial Dimension.

The result of ANOVA (Regression Analysis) test indicates significant at 0.01 level. The result from Table 5.14 indicates there is high degree of impact of all eight "Influencing Factors" together influence on Financial Dimension. So, Null Hypothesis is rejected.

The t-test values of "Inflation Rate", "Value of the U.S. Dollar", "Consumption of Gold", "Gold demand and supply" and "REPO Rate" are significant at 0.01 level. The results from Table 5.14 related to t-test indicate there is high degree of impact of "Inflation Rate", "Value of the U.S. Dollar", "Consumption of Gold", "Gold demand and supply" and "REPO Rate" on "Financial Dimension". So, Null Hypothesis is rejected.

Table – 5.14

Summary of "Financial Dimension" – "Factors influencing the volatility" Multiple Regression Analysis (Stock Brokers)

Highlights of Multiple Regression Analysis

DepVar: Financial Dimension, N: 54, Multiple R: 0.532, Squared multiple R: 0.187, Adjusted squared multiple R: 0.153, Standard error of estimate: 0.855

Summary of Multiple Regression Analysis

Effect	Coeff	Std Error	StdCoeff	Tolerance	t
Constant	5.756	1.513	0.000	.	3.805
Global Crisis	-0.050	0.051	-0.086	0.356	-0.782
Inflation Rate	0.055	0.071	0.065	0.591	0.771
Value of the U.S. Dollar	0.276	0.105	0.325	0.286	2.662**
Interest Rates	0.167	0.088	0.253	0.252	1.905
Consumption of Gold	0.132	0.086	0.151	0.553	1.551
Recession in world market	-0.130	0.055	-0.190	0.682	-2.509*
Gold demand and supply	-0.261	0.073	-0.293	0.653	-3.600**
REPO Rate	-0.055	0.076	-0.056	0.693	-0.582

***Significant at 0.05 level, **Significant at 0.01 level**

Analysis of Variance (ANOVA)

Source	Sum-of-Squares	df	Mean-Square	F-ratio
Regression	31.337	4	3.917	5.583**
Residual	136.558	49	0.715	

****Significant at 0.01 level**

Test for Existence of Correlation Amongst the Error Terms

Durbin-Watson D Statistic = 1.700***; First Order Autocorrelation = 0.155

***Not significant at 0.05 level, where the null hypothesis (Ho) involved was "there is no correlation amongst the residual (error) terms in the regression model". The null hypothesis was not rejected. Thus, absence of correlation and error terms cancelling each other is proved.

Source: Compiled By the Researcher

5.2.3.13 Analysis related to "Functional Dimension" - "Factors influencing the volatility" Multiple Regression Analysis (Total Sample)

Multiple Regression Analysis was employed and the summary of the result shown in the Table No. 5.15. Investors in Gold Futures, Gold dealers and Stock Brokers were the respondents who have given the valuable impressions regarding factors influencing the volatility.

H_{01}: Eight Factors together do not influence the functional dimension.

Or,

Mathematically, ***H_{01}***: *[The influence of eight factors on functional dimension] = 0*

The above hypothesis (H_{01}) was tested under two categories namely ANOVA Test (Regression Analysis) and t-test. ANOVA Test (Regression Analysis) was employed to confirm about eight Influencing Factors together influence the Functional Dimension. Similarly, t-test was executed to confirm about individual factors that influence Functional Dimension.

The result of ANOVA (Regression Analysis) test indicates significant at 0.01 level. The result from Table 5.15 indicates, there is high degree of impact of all eight "Influencing Factors" together on "Functional Dimension". So, Null Hypothesis is rejected.

The t-test values of "Inflation Rate", "Value of the U.S. Dollar", "Interest Rates", "Consumption of Gold", "Recession in world market" "Gold demand and supply" and "REPO Rate" are significant at 0.01 level. The results from Table 5.15 related to t-test indicate there is high degree of impact of all the above mentioned "Influencing Factors" individually on "Functional Dimension". So, Null Hypothesis is rejected.

The results from table no 5.15 indicates Adjusted squared multiple R: 0.349, Standard error of estimate: 0.905, the Durbin-Watson D Statistic = 2.030and First Order Autocorrelation = 0.016 and F-ratio is 91.176.

Table 5.15
Summary of Analysis related to "Functional Dimension" - "Factors influencing the volatility" Multiple Regression Analysis (Total Sample)

Highlights of Multiple Regression Analysis

DepVar: Functional Dimension, N: 630, Multiple R: 0.593 Squared multiple R: 0.352, Adjusted squared multiple R: 0.349, Standard error of estimate: 0.905

Summary of Multiple Regression Analysis

Effect	Coeff	Std Error	StdCoeff	Tolerance	T
Constant	-3.285	0.516	0.000	.	-7.893
Global Crisis	-0.171	0.022	-0.388	0.275	-7.937**
Inflation Rate	0.251	0.025	0.365	0.505	10.100**
Value of the U.S. Dollar	0.815	0.055	0.802	0.338	18.178**
Interest Rates	0.565	0.039	0.497	0.367	11.757**
Consumption of Gold	0.525	0.035	0.618	0.395	15.107**
Recession in world market	-0.350	0.025	-0.551	0.655	-15.117**
Gold demand and supply	-0.228	0.030	-0.299	0.521	-7.562**
REPO Rate	0.256	0.036	0.217	0.712	7.136**

****Significant at 0.01 level**

Analysis of Variance (ANOVA)

Source	Sum-of-Squares	Df	Mean-Square	F-ratio
Regression	595.653	8	75.555	91.176**
Residual	655.937	621	0.817	

****Significant at 0.01 level**

Test for Existence of Correlation Amongst the Error Terms

Durbin-Watson D Statistic = 2.030***; First Order Autocorrelation = 0.016

***Not significant at 0.05 level, where the null hypothesis (Ho) involved was "there is no correlation amongst the residual (error) terms in the regression model". The null hypothesis was not rejected. Thus, absence of correlation and error terms cancelling each other is proved.

Source: Compiled By the Researcher

5.2.3.14 Analysis related to "Demographic Dimension" - "Factors influencing the volatility" Multiple Regression Analysis (Total Sample)

Multiple Regression Analysis was employed and the summary of the result shown in the Table No. 5.16. Investors in Gold Futures, Gold dealers and Stock Brokers were the respondents who have given the valuable impressions regarding influencing factors of volatility on dimensions of gold futures.

H_{02}: Eight Factors together do not influence the demographic dimension.

Or,

Mathematically, $\boldsymbol{H_{02}}$: *[The influence of eight factors on demographic dimension] = 0*

The above hypothesis (H_{02}) was tested under two categories namely ANOVA Test (Regression Analysis) and t-test. ANOVA Test (Regression Analysis) was employed to confirm about eight Influencing Factors together influence on Demographic Dimension. Similarly, t-test was executed to confirm about individual Influencing Factor that influence on Demographic Dimension.

The result of ANOVA (Regression Analysis) test indicates significant at 0.01 level. The result from Table 5.16 indicates the high degree of impact of all eight factors "Global Crisis", "Inflation Rate", "Value of the U.S. Dollar", "Interest Rates", "Consumption of Gold", "Recession in world market" "Gold demand and supply" and "REPO Rate" together on "Demographic Dimension". So, Null Hypothesis is rejected.

The t-test values of "Consumption of Gold" and "Gold demand and supply" are significant at 0.01 level. The results from Table 5.16 related to t-test indicate there is high degree of impact of "Consumption of Gold" and "Gold demand and supply" individually on "Demographic Dimension". So, Null Hypothesis is rejected.

Table 5.16
Summary of "Demographic Dimension" - "Factors influencing the volatility" Multiple Regression Analysis (Total Sample)

Highlights of Multiple Regression Analysis

DepVar: Demographic Dimension, N: 630, Multiple R: 0.508, Squared multiple R: 0.258, Adjusted squared multiple R: 0.251, Standard error of estimate: 0.178

Summary of Multiple Regression Analysis

Effect	Coeff	Std Error	StdCoeff	Tolerance	T
Constant	1.238	0.552	0.000	.	2.285
Global Crisis	-0.065	0.028	-0.135	0.275	-2.297*
Inflation Rate	0.152	0.032	0.188	0.505	5.368
Value of the U.S. Dollar	0.033	0.058	0.030	0.338	0.561
Interest Rates	0.060	0.051	0.059	0.367	1.165
Consumption of Gold	0.135	0.055	0.155	0.395	2.967**
Recession in world market	-0.053	0.032	-0.050	0.655	-1.323
Gold demand and supply	0.355	0.039	0.513	0.521	8.753
REPO Rate	0.067	0.057	0.052	0.712	1.532

***Significant at 0.05 level, **Significant at 0.01 level**

Analysis of Variance (ANOVA)

Source	Sum-of-Squares	Df	Mean-Square	F-ratio
Regression	381.621	8	57.703	35.381**
Residual	1,097.599	621	1.387	

****Significant at 0.01 level**

Test for Existence of Correlation Amongst the Error Terms

Durbin-Watson D Statistic = 1.866.***; First Order Autocorrelation = 0.066

***Not significant at 0.05 level, where the null hypothesis (Ho) involved was "there is no correlation amongst the residual (error) terms in the regression model". The null hypothesis was not rejected. Thus, absence of correlation and error terms cancelling each other is proved.

Source: Compiled By the Researcher

The summary of results from Table 5.16 related to each causal factor and its influence on Demographic Dimension is given bellow:

As indicated by the ANOVA all the independent variables do influence dependent variable (Demographic Dimension). The F-ratio of Demographic Dimension and Influencing Factors is 35.381 which is significant at 0.01 level. Therefore, the Regression Model is valid.

The influence of the error terms as indicated by this is negligible. The null hypothesis involved there is no correlation among the residual error terms in the regression model. The error terms i.e., positive error cancels negative error.

Both of these together indicate the regression model is valid. Since the Regression Model is valid, the further analysis employed and the degree of influence of all variables put together is 25.1% as indicated by the Adjusted Squired Multiple Regression.

Consumption of Gold actually has the real influence in the dependent variable (Demographic Dimension), because the result of t-value is 2.967 which is significant at 0.01 level

Consumption of Gold actually have the real influence on dependent variable (Demographic Dimension) because the result shows un-standardized Coefficient is 0.135 and standardized coefficient is 0.155 which are moderate uphill (positive) linear relationship, the t-value is 2.987 significant at 0.01 level.

The negative value indicates the negative influence towards dependent variables. The negative results indicate the reverse conceptual aspect of understanding the term "Global Crisis". As indicated the result of t-value is -2.297 which is significant at 0.05 level but influence negatively, this can be stated as if Global Crisis increases the Demographic Dimension comes down.

5.2.3.15 Analysis related to "Opportunity Dimension" - "Factors influencing the volatility" Multiple Regression Analysis (Total Sample)

Multiple Regression Analysis was employed and the summary of the result shown in the Table No. 5.17. Investors in Gold Futures, Gold dealers and Stock Brokers were the respondents who have given the valuable impressions regarding influencing factors of volatility on dimensions of gold futures.

H_{03}: Eight Factors together do not influence the opportunity dimension.

Or,

Mathematically, $\boldsymbol{H_{03}}$: *[The influence of eight factors on opportunity dimension] = 0*

The above hypothesis (H_{03}) was tested under two categories namely ANOVA Test (Regression Analysis) and t-test. ANOVA Test (Regression Analysis) was employed to confirm about eight Influencing Factors together influence on Opportunity Dimension. Similarly, t-test was executed to confirm about all influencing factors individually influence on Opportunity Dimension.

The result of ANOVA (Regression Analysis) test indicates significant at 0.01 level. The result from Table 5.17 indicates there is high degree of impact of all eight "Influencing Factors" together influence on Opportunity Dimension. So, Null Hypothesis is rejected.

The t-test values of "Inflation Rate", "Value of the U.S. Dollar", "Consumption of Gold", "Recession in world market" "Gold demand and supply" and "REPO Rate" are significant at 0.01 level. The results from Table 5.17 related to t-test indicate there is high degree of impact of "Inflation Rate", "Value of the U.S. Dollar", "Consumption of Gold", "Recession in world market" "Gold demand and supply" and "REPO Rate" on "Opportunity Dimension". So, Null Hypothesis is rejected.

Table 5.17
Summary of "Opportunity Dimension" - "Factors influencing the volatility" Multiple Regression Analysis (Total Sample)

Highlights of Multiple Regression Analysis

DepVar: Opportunity Dimension, N: 630, Multiple R: 0.587, Squared multiple R: 0.237
Adjusted squared multiple R: 0.228 Standard error of estimate: 1.126

Summary of Multiple Regression Analysis

Effect	Coeff	Std Error	StdCoeff	Tolerance	T
Constant	2.531	0.518	0.000	.	5.886
Global Crisis	-0.068	0.027	-0.150	0.275	-2.525*
Inflation Rate	0.229	0.031	0.323	0.505	7.390
Value of the U.S. Dollar	0.175	0.056	0.167	0.338	3.127**
Interest Rates	0.200	0.059	0.208	0.367	5.066**
Consumption of Gold	0.510	0.053	0.570	0.395	9.585**
Recession in world market	-0.209	0.031	-0.262	0.655	-6.770**
Gold demand and supply	-0.138	0.038	-0.176	0.521	-3.678**
REPO Rate	-0.195	0.055	-0.160	0.712	-5.355**

***Significant at 0.05 level, **Significant at 0.01 level**

Analysis of Variance (ANOVA)

Source	Sum-of-Squares	Df	Mean-Square	F-ratio
Regression	310.527	8	38.816	30.671**
Residual	1,001.072	621	1.266	

****Significant at 0.01 level**

Test for Existence of Correlation Amongst the Error Terms

Durbin-Watson D Statistic = 1.905***; First Order Autocorrelation = 0.057

***Not significant at 0.05 level, where the null hypothesis (Ho) involved was "there is no correlation amongst the residual (error) terms in the regression model". The null hypothesis was not rejected. Thus, absence of correlation and error terms cancelling each other is proved.

Source: Compiled By the Researcher

5.2.3.16 Analysis related to "Financial Dimension" - "Factors influencing the volatility" Multiple Regression Analysis (Total Sample)

Multiple Regression Analysis was employed and the summary of the result shown in the Table No. 5.18. Investors in Gold Futures, Gold dealers and Stock Brokers were the respondents who have given the valuable impressions regarding influencing factors of volatility on dimensions of gold futures.

H_{04}: The Eight Factors together do not influence the financial dimension.

Or,

Mathematically, $\boldsymbol{H_{04}}$: *[The influence of eight factors on financial dimension] = 0*

The above hypothesis (H_{04}) was tested under two categories namely ANOVA Test (Regression Analysis) and t-test. ANOVA Test (Regression Analysis) was employed to confirm about eight Influencing Factors together influence on Financial Dimension. Similarly, t-test was executed to confirm about all influencing factors individually influence on Financial Dimension.

The result of ANOVA (Regression Analysis) test indicates significant at 0.01 level. The result from Table 5.18 indicates there is high degree of impact of all eight "Influencing Factors" together influence on Financial Dimension. So, Null Hypothesis is rejected.

The t-test values of "Inflation Rate", "Value of the U.S. Dollar", "Consumption of Gold", "Gold demand and supply" and "REPO Rate" are significant at 0.01 level. The results from Table 5.18 related to t-test indicate there is high degree of impact of "Inflation Rate", "Value of the U.S. Dollar", "Consumption of Gold", "Gold demand and supply" and "REPO Rate" on "Financial Dimension". So, Null Hypothesis is rejected.

The results from table no 5.18 indicates Adjusted squared multiple R: 0.295, Standard error of estimate: 0.905, the Durbin-Watson D Statistic = 2.030and First Order Autocorrelation = 0.016 and F-ratio is 52.526.

Table 5.18

Summary of "Financial Dimension" - "Factors influencing the volatility" Multiple Regression Analysis (Total Sample)

Highlights of Multiple Regression Analysis

DepVar: Financial Dimension, N: 630, Multiple R: 0.558 Squared multiple R: 0.301
Adjusted squared multiple R: 0.295, Standard error of estimate: 1.161

Summary of Multiple Regression Analysis

Effect	Coeff	Std Error	StdCoeff	Tolerance	T
Constant	0.672	0.535	0.000	.	1.257
Global Crisis	-0.005	0.028	-0.010	0.275	-0.169
Inflation Rate	0.100	0.032	0.131	0.505	3.131**
Value of the U.S. Dollar	0.561	0.058	0.598	0.338	9.733**
Interest Rates	0.260	0.051	0.252	0.367	5.127**
Consumption of Gold	0.266	0.055	0.283	0.395	5.963**
Recession in world market	-0.153	0.032	-0.167	0.655	-5.598**
Gold demand and supply	-0.065	0.039	-0.075	0.521	-1.651
REPO Rate	-0.172	0.056	-0.131	0.712	-3.727**

****Significant at 0.01 level**

Analysis of Variance (ANOVA)

Source	Sum-of-Squares	Df	Mean-Square	F-ratio
Regression	558.625	8	57.328	52.526**
Residual	1,066.315	621	1.358	

****Significant at 0.01 level**

Test for Existence of Correlation Amongst the Error Terms

Durbin-Watson D Statistic = 1.697***; First Order Autocorrelation = 0.151

***Not significant at 0.05 level, where the null hypothesis (Ho) involved was "there is no correlation amongst the residual (error) terms in the regression model". The null hypothesis was not rejected. Thus, absence of correlation and error terms cancelling each other is proved.

Source: Compiled By the Researcher

5.2.4Analysis regarding comparison summary of percentage of Adjusted Squared Multiple Regression Analysis with respect to different Category of Respondents

The overall picture is shown in the Table No. 5.19 regarding the comparison summary of percentage of Adjusted Squared Multiple Regression Analysis with respect to different Category of Respondents (Investors of Gold Futures, Gold Dealers and Total Respondents).

5.2.4.1 The result of Adjusted Squared Multiple Regression Analysis among different categories of respondents with reference to "Functional Dimension"

The result of Adjusted Squared Multiple Regression Analysis is 0.479 with respect to Investors of Gold Futures and indicating that 47.9% of the variability in the response is explained by the exploratory variable. Investors of Gold Futures feel all the Independent Variables ("Global Crisis", "Inflation Rate", "Value of the U.S. Dollar", "Interest Rates", "Consumption of Gold", "Recession in world market", "Gold demand and supply" and "REPO Rate") and Dependent Variables ("Functional Dimension", "Demographic Dimension", "Opportunity Dimension" and "Financial Dimension") are the most useful variables to fit a curve or line.

The result of Adjusted Squared Multiple Regression Analysis is 0.005 with respect to Gold Dealers and indicating that 0.5% of the variability which is very low in the response is explained by the exploratory variable. Gold Dealers feel all the Independent Variables ("Global Crisis", "Inflation Rate", "Value of the U.S. Dollar", "Interest Rates", "Consumption of Gold", "Recession in world market", "Gold demand and supply" and "REPO Rate") and Dependent Variables ("Functional Dimension", "Demographic Dimension", "Opportunity Dimension" and "Financial Dimension") are not the useful variables to fit a curve or line.

The result of Adjusted Squared Multiple Regression Analysis is 0.559 with respect to Stock Brokers and indicating that 55.9% of the variability which is very high in the response is explained by the exploratory variable. Stock Brokers feel all the Independent Variables ("Global Crisis", "Inflation Rate", "Value of the U.S. Dollar", "Interest Rates",

"Consumption of Gold", "Recession in world market", "Gold demand and supply" and "REPO Rate") and Dependent Variables ("Functional Dimension", "Demographic Dimension", "Opportunity Dimension" and "Financial Dimension") are most useful variables to fit a curve or line.

As indicated in the table no. 5.19, the percentage of adjusted squared multiple regression analysis among different category of respondents in which Investors of Gold Futures feel there is great impact of "Influencing Factors" towards "Dimensions of Gold Futures" but Gold Dealersfeel there is no impact of "Influencing Factors" towards "Dimensions of Gold Futures".

5.2.4.2 The results of Adjusted Squared Multiple Regression Analysis among different categories of respondents with reference to Demographic Dimension

The result of Adjusted Squared Multiple Regression Analysis is 0.215with respect to Investors of Gold Futures and indicating that 21.5% of the variability in the response is explained by the exploratory variable. Investors of Gold Futures feel all the Independent Variables ("Global Crisis", "Inflation Rate", "Value of the U.S. Dollar", "Interest Rates", "Consumption of Gold", "Recession in world market", "Gold demand and supply" and "REPO Rate") and Dependent Variables ("Functional Dimension", "Demographic Dimension", "Opportunity Dimension" and "Financial Dimension") are the most useful variables to fit a curve or line.

The result of Adjusted Squared Multiple Regression Analysis is 0.107with respect to Gold Dealers and indicating that 10.7 % of the variability which is very low in the response is explained by the exploratory variable. Gold Dealers feel all the Independent Variables ("Global Crisis", "Inflation Rate", "Value of the U.S. Dollar", "Interest Rates", "Consumption of Gold", "Recession in world market", "Gold demand and supply" and "REPO Rate") and Dependent Variables ("Functional Dimension", "Demographic Dimension", "Opportunity Dimension" and "Financial Dimension") are not the useful variables to fit a curve or line.

The result of Adjusted Squared Multiple Regression Analysis is 0.051 with respect to Stock Brokers and indicating that 5.1% of the variability in the response is explained by the exploratory variable. Stock Brokers feel all the Independent Variables ("Global Crisis", "Inflation Rate", "Value of the U.S. Dollar", "Interest Rates", "Consumption of Gold", "Recession in world market", "Gold demand and supply" and "REPO Rate") and Dependent Variables ("Functional Dimension", "Demographic Dimension", "Opportunity Dimension" and "Financial Dimension") are not the useful variables to fit a curve or line.

As indicated in the table no. 5.19, the percentage of adjusted squared multiple regression analysis among different category of respondents in which Investors of Gold Futures feel there is great impact of "Influencing Factors" towards "Dimensions of Gold Futures" but Gold Dealers feel there is no impact of "Influencing Factors" towards "Dimensions of Gold Futures".

5.2.4.3 The results of Adjusted Squared Multiple Regression Analysis among different categories of respondents with reference to Opportunity Dimension

The result of Adjusted Squared Multiple Regression Analysis is 0.265 with respect to Investors of Gold Futures and indicating that 26.5% of the variability in the response is explained by the exploratory variable.

Investors of Gold Futures feel all the Independent Variables ("Global Crisis", "Inflation Rate", "Value of the U.S. Dollar", "Interest Rates", "Consumption of Gold", "Recession in world market", "Gold demand and supply" and "REPO Rate") and Dependent Variables ("Functional Dimension", "Demographic Dimension", "Opportunity Dimension" and "Financial Dimension") are the most useful variables to fit a curve or line.

The result of Adjusted Squared Multiple Regression Analysis is 0.176 with respect to Gold Dealers and indicating that 17.6% of the variability which is very low in the response is explained by the exploratory variable. Gold Dealers feel all the Independent Variables ("Global Crisis", "Inflation Rate", "Value of the U.S. Dollar", "Interest Rates", "Consumption of Gold", "Recession in world market", "Gold demand and supply" and "REPO Rate") and Dependent Variables ("Functional Dimension", "Demographic

Dimension", "Opportunity Dimension" and "Financial Dimension") are not the useful variables to fit a curve or line.

The result of Adjusted Squared Multiple Regression Analysis is 0.278 with respect to Stock Brokers and indicating that 27.8% of the variability in the response is explained by the exploratory variable. Investors of Gold Futures feel all the Independent Variables ("Global Crisis", "Inflation Rate", "Value of the U.S. Dollar", "Interest Rates", "Consumption of Gold", "Recession in world market", "Gold demand and supply" and "REPO Rate") and Dependent Variables ("Functional Dimension", "Demographic Dimension", "Opportunity Dimension" and "Financial Dimension") are the most useful variables to fit a curve or line.

As indicated in the table no. 5.19, the percentage of adjusted squared multiple regression analysis among different category of respondents in which Investors of Gold Futures and Stock Brokers feel there is great impact of "Influencing Factors" towards "Dimensions of Gold Futures" but Gold Dealers feel there is no impact of "Influencing Factors" towards "Dimensions of Gold Futures".

5.2.4.4 The results Adjusted Squared Multiple Regression Analysis among different categories of respondents with reference to Financial Dimension

The result of Adjusted Squared Multiple Regression Analysis is 0.372 with respect to Investors of Gold Futures and indicating that 37.2% of the variability in the response is explained by the exploratory variable. Investors of Gold Futures feel all the Independent Variables ("Global Crisis", "Inflation Rate", "Value of the U.S. Dollar", "Interest Rates", "Consumption of Gold", "Recession in world market", "Gold demand and supply" and "REPO Rate") and Dependent Variables ("Functional Dimension", "Demographic Dimension", "Opportunity Dimension" and "Financial Dimension") are the most useful variables to fit a curve or line.

The result of Adjusted Squared Multiple Regression Analysis is 0.222 with respect to Gold Dealers and indicating that 22.2% of the variability which is moderate in the response is explained by the exploratory variable. Gold Dealers feel all the Independent

Variables ("Global Crisis", "Inflation Rate", "Value of the U.S. Dollar", "Interest Rates", "Consumption of Gold", "Recession in world market", "Gold demand and supply" and "REPO Rate") and Dependent Variables ("Functional Dimension", "Demographic Dimension", "Opportunity Dimension" and "Financial Dimension") are the useful variables to fit a curve or line.

The result of Adjusted Squared Multiple Regression Analysis is 0.153 with respect to Stock Brokers and indicating that 15.3% of the variability which is very low in the response is explained by the exploratory variable. Stock Brokers feel all the Independent Variables ("Global Crisis", "Inflation Rate", "Value of the U.S. Dollar", "Interest Rates", "Consumption of Gold", "Recession in world market", "Gold demand and supply" and "REPO Rate") and Dependent Variables ("Functional Dimension", "Demographic Dimension", "Opportunity Dimension" and "Financial Dimension") are not the useful variables to fit a curve or line.

As indicated in the table no. 5.19, the percentage of adjusted squared multiple regression analysis among different category of respondents in which Investors of Gold Futures and Stock Brokers feel there is great impact of "Influencing Factors" towards "Dimensions of Gold Futures" but Gold Dealers feel there is no impact of "Influencing Factors" towards "Dimensions of Gold Futures".

Table – 5.19
Comparison of Percentage (%) of "Adjusted Squared Multiple R" Among Different Category of Respondents

Category of Respondents	Dimensions of Gold Futures			
	Functional Dimension	**Demographic Dimension**	**Opportunity Dimension**	**Financial Dimension**
Investors of Gold Futures	47.90	21.50	26.50	37.20
Gold Dealers	0.50	10.70	17.60	22.20
Stock Brokers	55.90	5.10	27.80	15.30
Total	34.90	25.10	22.80	29.50

Source: Compiled By the Researcher

5.2.5 Various risks in investing gold and need to be addressed in view of the volatility

Based the result from table no 5.20, most of the expert of stock market, gold dealers and investors of gold futures indicated the most common risk in gold investment are Price Risk, Exchange Rate Risk and Bankruptcy of Bank and the Frequency of Occurrence in Percentage are 20%, 16% and 13% respectively. Similarly, Trading Interruptions, Operational Risk, Identity Theft, Insurance Exclusions, Termination of Gold Republic, Laws and Regulations, Modern Portfolio Theory, Options and Volatility Index Indicator are also consider as the risk of investing in gold.

Table - 5.20

Various risks in investing gold and need to be addressed in view of the volatility. (Based on Responses to Semi-Structured Interview Schedule)

SL. No.	Financial Problems of Export Marketing	Frequency of Occurrence in Percentage
1	Price Risk	20
2	Exchange Rate Risk	16
3	Bankruptcy of Bank	13
5	Trading Interruptions	12
5	Operational Risk	10
6	Identity Theft	8
7	Insurance Exclusions	6
8	Termination of Gold Republic	5
9	Laws and Regulations	5
10	Modern Portfolio Theory	3
11	Options	2
12	Volatility Index Indicator	1

Source: Compiled By the Researcher

Graph - 5.3

Risks in investing gold and need to be addressed in view of the volatility.

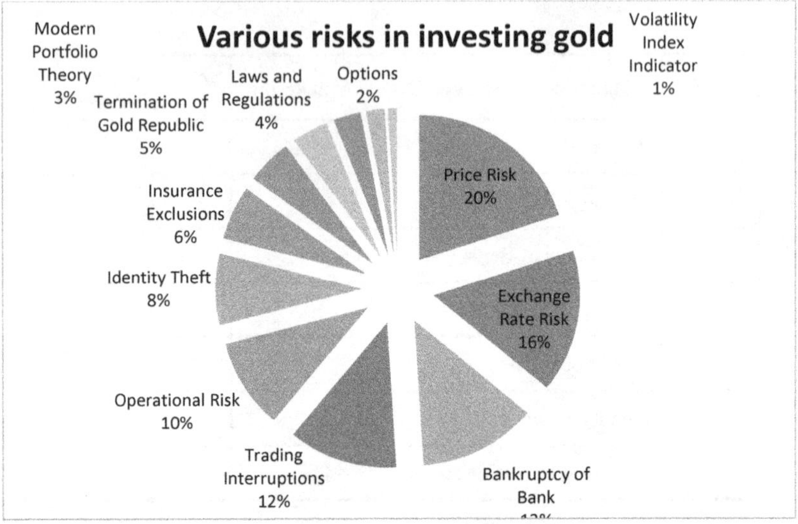

5.2.6 The hedging mechanism to counter various risks associated with volatility.

Analysis based on the objective no. 3 the hedging mechanism to counter various risks associated with volatility. The experts and stock market practitioners have given their valuable opinion and the most frequent opinion occurrence predominantly regarding dimensions of Gold Futures with special reference to bullion market. Table 5.21 shows the hedging mechanism to counter various risks associated with volatility.

Hedging Mechanism counter various risks associated with volatility includes Stocks, Exchange-traded funds, Insurance, Forward contracts, Swaps, Options, Over-the-counter and Futures contracts.

Securities include investments in shares, equities, indices, etc. The risk associated with these securities is known as "Equity Risk" or "Securities Risk". Brokers sell securities and commodities directly to individual clients. They advise people on appropriate investments based on the client's needs and financial ability.

Table - 5.21
The hedging mechanism to counter various risks associated with volatility.(Based on Responses to Semi-Structured Interview Schedule)

SL. No.	Hedging mechanism to counter various risks	Frequency of Occurrence in Percentage
1	Stocks	25
2	Exchange-traded funds	19
3	Insurance	15
5	Forward contracts	12
5	Swaps	10
6	Options	8
7	Over-the-counter	7
8	Futures contracts	5

Source: Compiled By the Researcher

Graph - 5.4

The hedging mechanism to counter various risks associated with volatility.

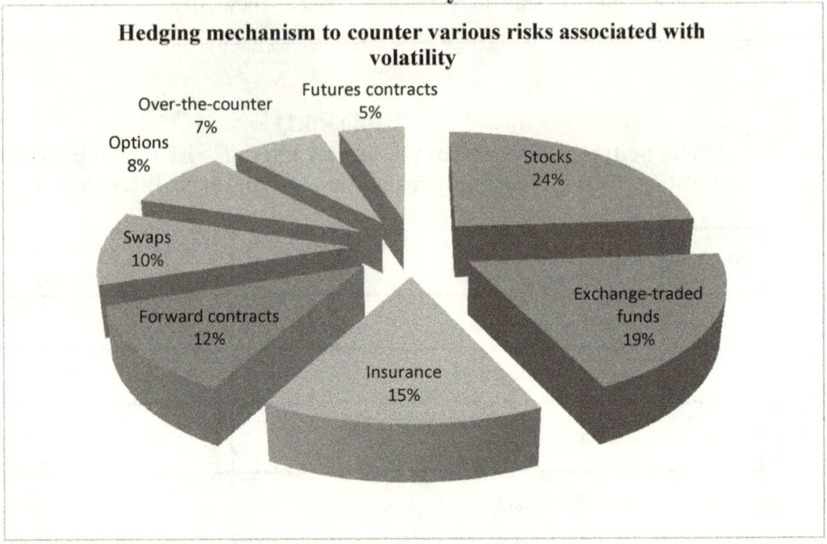

5.2.7 Analysis based on compare and contrasts the dimensions of commodity futures of bullion market of select Western markets with India

The Indian market for gold and silver has become an enormous source of fascination for the western market. One cannot help but notice the huge number of articles by analysts focusing on seasonal buying patterns, Diwali festival purchases, weddings, the extent of monsoon rains, dowry, "good" Hindu dates and so on. The heightened level of interest in India has become evident in many parts of the industry and now gold producers are even willing to spend a considerable amount of money sponsoring dedicated research projects the latest example being the study undertaken by Grendon International Research &Virtual Metals to enhance their understanding of the Indian bullion market and how it might develop.

Virtually everybody attending this forum is aware of the massive acceleration in gold imports that followed the liberalization measures adopted through the 1990s. Similarly, most are also aware that this trend stalled towards the end of the decade and then fell significantly last year and continues to be very weak in 2003.

Most market analysts tend to concentrate on the cultural reasons why Indians buy gold, such as for weddings, festivals, and so on. However, often behind these cultural norms is a genuine rationale. There is no doubt that in India gold and silver were actually proper, rational, financial assets for many purchasers, against a background of high rates of inflation and rapid depreciation of the rupee. In an environment where there were few ways to hedge those risks, gold and silver would probably be the only ways in which many private investors around the country could do so. But now those needs are in decline. We have seen a rapid fall off in inflation in India, as we have seen around the world, and we have also seen greater rupee stability over time. This significantly reduces two of the major drivers for demand at least, if not directly at least in terms of the subconscious.

Table - 5.22

The compare and contrasts the dimensions of commodity futures of bullion market of selected Western markets with India

Name of the Country	Population (In Crore)	Gold Reserve (Tonnes)	Foreign Reserve (%)
USA	32.34	8,133.50	75.20%
Germany	8.27	3,371.00	70.60%
France	6.69	2,436.00	63.90%
Switzerland	8.42	1040	54.20%
India	132.42	560.3	5.50%

The volatility linkage analyses confirm the existence of volatility transmission among the majority of the sample countries' gold futures. The data so collected from various sources related to compare and contrast the Risks of commodity futures of bullion market of select Western markets with India. The three main areas of commodities are food, energy, and metals. The most popular food futures are for meat, wheat, and sugar. Most energy futures are for oil and gasoline.

Graph - 5.5

Graph shows the comparison of Population of selected Western markets with India

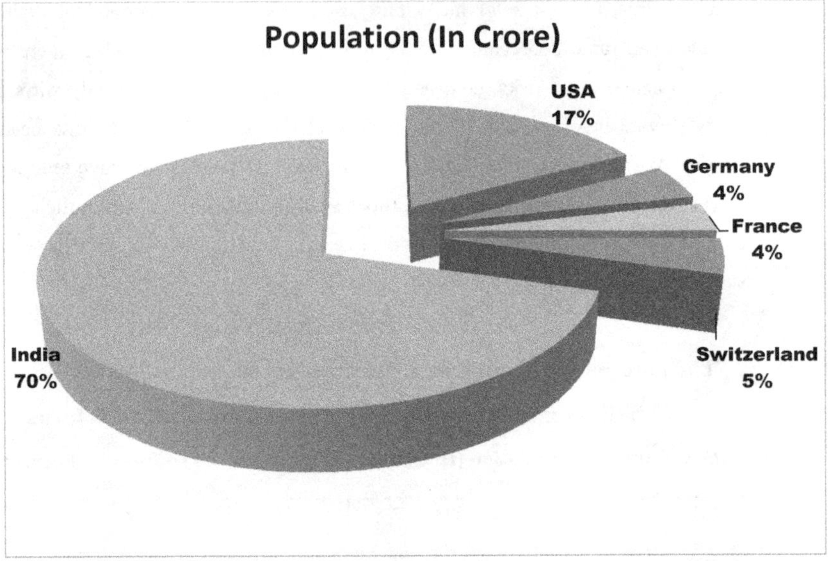

Metals using futures include gold, silver, and copper. The results are the risks of commodity futures of bullion market of Western markets such as USA, Germany, France and Switzerland with India.

Graph - 5.6
Graph shows the comparison of Gold Reserveof selected Western markets with India

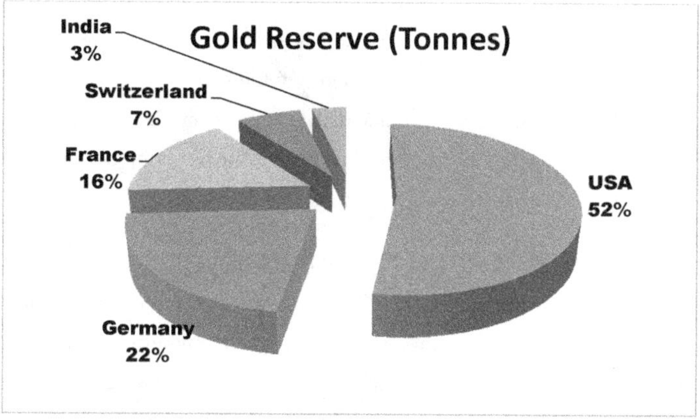

India is the country with maximum population i.e., 132.42 crores but minimum Gold Reserve of 560.3 tonnes and only 5.5% of foreign reserves.

Graph - 5.7
Graph shows the comparison of Percentage of Foreign Reserve of selected Western markets with India

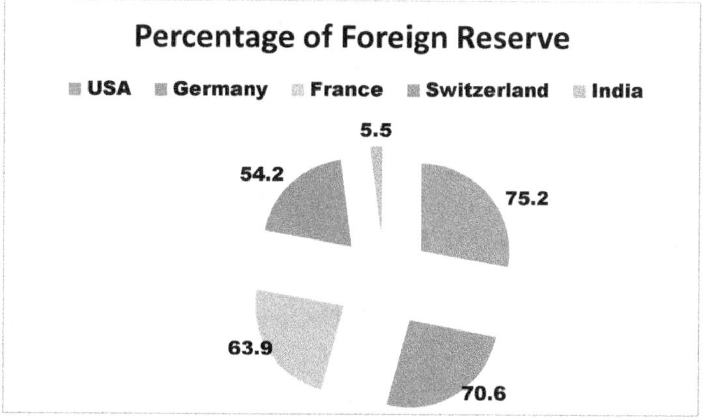

In case of USA, the population 32.34 crores with maximum Gold Reserve of 8,133.5 tonnes and 75.2% of foreign reserves.

In case of Germany, the population 8.27 crores with Gold Reserve of 3,371.0 tonnes and 70.6% of foreign reserves. And in case of France, the population 6.69 crores with the Gold Reserve of 2,436.0 tonnes and 63.9% of foreign reserves.

Based on the above result, the commodity futures of bullion market of Western markets are highly risk comparable to Indian market. India is market for the commodity futures of bullion market with good opportunities for the Investors in Gold Futures as well as for the Gold Dealers.

5.3 SUMMARY OF DATA ANALYSIS

5.3.1 Factors influencing the volatility in the bullion market with respect to gold

The commonly observed influencing factors of volatility in the bullion market are "Global Crisis", "Inflation Rate", "Value of the U.S. Dollar", "Interest Rates", "Consumption of Gold", "Recession in world market" "Gold demand and supply" and "REPO Rate". "Global Crisis" is the factor that influences the volatility in the bullion market with respect to gold. The experts have given their first preferences around 21 percent of respondents. "Inflation Rate" is the factor that influences the volatility in the bullion market with respect to gold. The experts have given their first preferences around 18 percent of respondents. "Value of the U.S. Dollar" is the factor that influences the volatility in the bullion market with respect to gold. The experts have given their first preferences around 15 percent of respondents.

5.3.2 Common dimensions of Gold Futures with special reference to bullion market

The commonly observed dimensions of Gold Futures with special reference to bullion market are "Functional Dimension", "Demographic Dimension", "Opportunity Dimension" and "Financial Dimension". The experts' opinion summarizes the Industrial Usage and Individual Usage of gold that represent the "Functional Dimension" of gold futures. The Frequency of Occurrence in Percentage of Functional Dimension was31 percent with special reference to gold futures.

The experts' opinion summarizes the Degree of Savings and Long term investment plan related to gold that represent the "Demographic Dimension" of gold futures. The Frequency of Occurrence in Percentage of Demographic Dimension was27 percent with special reference to gold futures. The experts' opinion summarizes the Investment during times of economic instability, volatile commodity markets related to gold that represent the "Opportunity Dimension" of gold futures. The Frequency of Occurrence in Percentage of Opportunity Dimension was22 percent with special reference to gold futures. The experts' opinion summarizes the Resale Value and Loan against the gold related to gold that represent the "Financial Dimension" of gold futures. The Frequency of Occurrence in Percentage of Opportunity Dimension was20 percent with special reference to gold futures.

5.3.3 Analysis regarding comparison summary of percentage of Adjusted Squared Multiple Regression Analysis with respect to different Category of Respondents

The result of Adjusted Squared Multiple Regression Analysis is 0.479 with respect to Investors of Gold Futures and indicating that 47.9% of the variability in the response is explained by the exploratory variable. Investors of Gold Futures feel all the Independent Variables ("Global Crisis", "Inflation Rate", "Value of the U.S. Dollar", "Interest Rates", "Consumption of Gold", "Recession in world market", "Gold demand and supply" and "REPO Rate") and Dependent Variables ("Functional Dimension", "Demographic Dimension", "Opportunity Dimension" and "Financial Dimension") are the most useful variables to fit a curve or line.

5.3.4Various risks in investing gold and need to be addressed in view of the volatility

The analysis is based on the risks in investing gold and need to be addressed in view of the volatility. Based the result from table most of the expert of stock market, gold dealers and investors of gold futures indicated the most common risk in gold investment are Price Risk, Exchange Rate Risk and Bankruptcy of Bank and the Frequency of Occurrence in Percentage are 20%, 16% and 13% respectively. Similarly, Trading Interruptions, Operational Risk, Identity Theft, Insurance Exclusions, Termination of Gold Republic, Laws and Regulations, Modern Portfolio Theory, Options and Volatility Index Indicator are also consider as the risk of investing in gold.

5.3.5The hedging mechanism to counter various risks associated with volatility.

The experts and stock market practitioners have given their valuable opinion and the most frequent opinion occurrence predominantly regarding dimensions of Gold Futures with special reference to bullion market. Table shows the hedging mechanism to counter various risks associated with volatility. Hedging Mechanism counter various risks associated with volatility includes Stocks, Exchange-traded funds, Insurance, Forward contracts, Swaps, Options, Over-the-counter and Futures contracts. Securities include investments in shares, equities, indices, etc. The risk associated with these securities is known as "Equity Risk" or "Securities Risk". Brokers sell securities and commodities directly to individual clients. They advise people on appropriate investments based on the client's needs and financial ability.

5.3.6 Compare and contrast the dimensions of commodity futures of bullion market of select Western markets with India.

The volatility linkage analyses confirm the existence of volatility transmission among the majority of the sample countries' gold futures. The data so collected from various sources related to compare and contrast the Risks of commodity futures of bullion market of select Western markets with India. The three main areas of commodities are food, energy, and metals. The most popular food futures are for meat, wheat, and sugar. Most energy futures are for oil and gasoline.

Metals using futures include gold, silver, and copper. The results are the risks of commodity futures of bullion market of Western markets such as USA, Germany, France and Switzerland with India. India is the country with maximum population i.e., 132.42 crores but minimum Gold Reserve of 560.3 tonnes and only 5.5% of foreign reserves.

In case of USA, the population 32.34 crores with maximum Gold Reserve of 8,133.5 tonnes and 75.2% of foreign reserves.

In case of Germany, the population 8.27 crores with Gold Reserve of 3,371.0 tonnes and 70.6% of foreign reserves. And in case of France, the population 6.69 crores with the Gold Reserve of 2,436.0 tonnes and 63.9% of foreign reserves.

Based on the above result, the commodity futures of bullion market of Western markets are highly risk comparable to Indian market. India is market for the commodity futures of bullion market with good opportunities for the Investors in Gold Futures as well as for the Gold Dealers.

5.4 INTERPRETATION

The entire chapter is based on the summary of results and the attempt to explain the results by considering the practical realities, the previous works and the experts' opinions.

5.4.1 The interpretation based on summary of the results that contain various Factors influencing the volatility in the bullion market with respect to gold. The commonly observed influencing factors of volatility in the bullion market are "Global Crisis", "Inflation Rate", "Value of the U.S. Dollar", "Interest Rates", "Consumption of Gold", "Recession in world market" "Gold demand and supply" and "REPO Rate". "Global Crisis" is the factor that influences the volatility in the bullion market with respect to gold. The experts have given their first preferences around 21 percent of respondents. "Inflation Rate" is the factor that influences the volatility in the bullion market with respect to gold. The experts have given their first preferences around 18 percent of respondents. "Value of the U.S. Dollar" is the factor that influences the volatility in the bullion market with respect to gold. The experts have given their first preferences around 15 percent of respondents.

5.4.2 The interpretation based on summary of the results that include common dimensions of Gold Futures with special reference to bullion market. The commonly observed dimensions of Gold Futures with special reference to bullion market are "Functional Dimension", "Demographic Dimension", "Opportunity Dimension" and "Financial Dimension". The experts' opinion summarizes the Industrial Usage and Individual Usage of gold that represent the "Functional Dimension" of gold futures. The Frequency of Occurrence in Percentage of Functional Dimension was 31 percent with special reference to gold futures. The experts' opinion summarizes the Degree of Savings and Long term investment plan related to gold that represent the "Demographic

Dimension" of gold futures. The Frequency of Occurrence in Percentage of Demographic Dimension was 27 percent with special reference to gold futures. The experts' opinion summarizes the Investment during times of economic instability, volatile commodity markets related to gold that represent the "Opportunity Dimension" of gold futures. The Frequency of Occurrence in Percentage of Opportunity Dimension was 22 percent with special reference to gold futures. The experts' opinion summarizes the Resale Value and Loan against the gold related to gold that represent the "Financial Dimension" of gold futures. The Frequency of Occurrence in Percentage of Opportunity Dimension was 20 percent with special reference to gold futures.

5.4.3 The interpretation based on summary of the results that contain the degree of impact related to influencing factors of volatility on dimensions of gold futures.

As indicated by the ANOVA all the independent variables do influence dependent variable (Functional Dimension). The F-ratio of Functional Dimension and Influencing Factors is 72.551 which is significant at 0.01 level. Therefore, the Regression Model is valid. Since the Regression Model is valid, the further analysis employed and the degree of influence of all variables put together is 58.9% as indicated by the Adjusted Squired Multiple Regression. "Value of the U.S. Dollar"actually has the real influence in the dependent variable (Functional Dimension) because the result shows the t-value is 10.332 which is significant at 0.01 level. Remain independent variables can be arranged in the following order as they influence on dependent variable (Functional Dimension) based on the t-value (i) REPO Rate, (ii) Consumption of Gold, (iii) Interest Rates, (iv) Inflation Rate. The independent variable (REPO Rate) actually has the real influence on dependent variable (Functional Dimension) because the result shows the t-value is 6.551 which is significant at 0.01 level. The independent variable (Consumption of Gold) actually has the real influence on dependent variable (Functional Dimension) because the result shows the t-value is 6.315 which is significant at 0.01 level. The negative value indicates the negative influence of independent variable towards dependent variable. Following are the two variables that influence negatively: (i) Recession in world market and (ii) Gold demand and supply. The independent variable (Global Crisis) actually don't have any real influence on dependent variable (Functional Dimension) because the result shows the t-value is -1.829 which is not significant at 0.01 level.

The result of ANOVA (Regression Analysis) test indicates significant at 0.01 level. The result indicates there is high degree of impact of all eight "Export Problems" together on "Develop the relation with ultimate buyer". So, Null Hypothesis is rejected.

The t-test values of "Increases Global Crisis", "Market risks and Uncertainties", "Changes of Readymade Garments Design", "Recession in world market", "Changes of Technology", "Fluctuations in Exchange Rate", , "Unstable Political Environment" and "Lack of Infrastructure" are significant at 0.01 level. The results related to t-test indicate there is high degree of impact of all eight "Export Problems" together on "Develop the relation with ultimate buyer". So, Null Hypothesis is rejected.

5.4.4 The interpretation based on summary of the results that contain the Comparison summary of percentage of Adjusted Squared Multiple Regression Analysis with respect to different Category of Respondents.

The result of Adjusted Squared Multiple Regression Analysis is 0.479 with respect to Investors of Gold Futures and indicating that 47.9% of the variability in the response is explained by the exploratory variable. Investors of Gold Futures feel all the Independent Variables ("Global Crisis", "Inflation Rate", "Value of the U.S. Dollar", "Interest Rates", "Consumption of Gold", "Recession in world market", "Gold demand and supply" and "REPO Rate") and Dependent Variables ("Functional Dimension", "Demographic Dimension", "Opportunity Dimension" and "Financial Dimension") are the most useful variables to fit a curve or line. The result of Adjusted Squared Multiple Regression Analysis is 0.559 with respect to Stock Brokers and indicating that 55.90% of the variability in the response is explained by the exploratory variable. Stock Brokers feel all the Independent Variables ("Global Crisis", "Inflation Rate", "Value of the U.S. Dollar", "Interest Rates", "Consumption of Gold", "Recession in world market", "Gold demand and supply" and "REPO Rate") and Dependent Variables ("Functional Dimension", "Demographic Dimension", "Opportunity Dimension" and "Financial Dimension") are the most useful variables to fit a curve or line.

The result of Adjusted Squared Multiple Regression Analysis is 0.005 with respect to Gold Dealers and indicating that 0.5% of the variability which is very low in the response is explained by the exploratory variable. Gold Dealers feel all the Independent Variables ("Global Crisis", "Inflation Rate", "Value of the U.S. Dollar", "Interest Rates", "Consumption of Gold", "Recession in world market", "Gold demand and supply" and "REPO Rate") and Dependent Variables ("Functional Dimension", "Demographic Dimension", "Opportunity Dimension" and "Financial Dimension") are not the useful variables to fit a curve or line. As indicated in the table, the percentage of adjusted squared multiple regression analysis among different category of respondents in which Investors of Gold Futures and Stock Brokers feel there is great impact of "Influencing Factors" towards "Dimensions of Gold Futures" but Gold Dealers feel there is no impact of "Influencing Factors" towards "Dimensions of Gold Futures".

5.4.5 Various risks in investing gold and need to be addressed in view of the volatility. The analysis is based on risks in investing gold and need to be addressed in view of the volatility. Based the result from table, most of the expert of stock market, gold dealers and investors of gold futures indicated the most common risk in gold investment are Price Risk, Exchange Rate Risk and Bankruptcy of Bank and the Frequency of Occurrence in Percentage are 20%, 16% and 13% respectively. Similarly, Trading Interruptions, Operational Risk, Identity Theft, Insurance Exclusions, Termination of Gold Republic, Laws and Regulations, Modern Portfolio Theory, Options and Volatility Index Indicator are also consider as the risk of investing in gold.

5.4.6 The hedging mechanism to counter various risks associated with volatility. The experts and stock market practitioners have given their valuable opinion and the most frequent opinion occurrence predominantly regarding dimensions of Gold Futures with special reference to bullion market. Table shows the hedging mechanism to counter various risks associated with volatility. Hedging Mechanism counter various risks associated with volatility includes Stocks, Exchange-traded funds, Insurance, Forward contracts, Swaps, Options, Over-the-counter and Futures contracts. Securities include investments in shares, equities, indices, etc.

The risk associated with these securities is known as "Equity Risk" or "Securities Risk". Brokers sell securities and commodities directly to individual clients. They advise people on appropriate investments based on the client's needs and financial ability.

5.4.7 The volatility linkage analyses confirm the existence of volatility transmission among the majority of the sample countries' gold futures. The data so collected from various sources related to compare and contrast the Risks of commodity futures of bullion market of select Western markets with India. The three main areas of commodities are food, energy, and metals. The most popular food futures are for meat, wheat, and sugar. Most energy futures are for oil and gasoline.

Metals using futures include gold, silver, and copper. The results are the risks of commodity futures of bullion market of Western markets such as USA, Germany, France and Switzerland with India. India is the country with maximum population i.e., 132.42 crores but minimum Gold Reserve of 560.3 tonnes and only 5.5% of foreign reserves.

In case of USA, the population 32.34 crores with maximum Gold Reserve of 8,133.5 tonnes and 75.2% of foreign reserves.

In case of Germany, the population 8.27 crores with Gold Reserve of 3,371.0 tonnes and 70.6% of foreign reserves. And in case of France, the population 6.69 crores with the Gold Reserve of 2,436.0 tonnes and 63.9% of foreign reserves.

Based on the above result, the commodity futures of bullion market of Western markets are highly risk comparable to Indian market. India is market for the commodity futures of bullion market with good opportunities for the Investors in Gold Futures as well as for the Gold Dealers.

Table A.1

First Iteration of Delphi Technique with Respect to "Influencing Factors" of the volatility in the bullion market (No. of Experts = 10)

Sl. No.	Category	Details	Mean % Agreement	Remarks
Summary of First Iteration				
Sl. No.	**Category**	**Details**	**Mean % Agreement**	**Remarks**
1	Factors	Different Factors, and History	64.40	Disagreement on nature of "History" Factor
2	Items	35	65.12	Disagreement on "Span of Attention" of Respondents
3	"Normality" Conformance	Based on Pilot Study of 80 Ss	52.20	Normality not within agreeable limits
Summary of Second Iteration				
Sl. No.	**Category**	**Details**	**Mean % Agreement**	**Remarks**
1	Factors	Factors and History merged	72.20	"History" Factor Merged with Other Factors
2	Items	27	73.40	Common and Irrelevant Items Reduced
3	"Normality" Conformance	Based on Pilot Study of 80 Ss	60.70	Levels of Normality May be Improved
Summary of Third Iteration				
Sl. No.	**Category**	**Details**	**Mean % Agreement**	**Remarks**
1	Factors	Factors in the form of 8 Factors	87.40	Factors Further Refined to Maintain Distinction
2	Items	22	88.40	Common and Irrelevant Items Further Reduced
3	"Normality" Conformance	Based on Pilot Study of 80 Ss	82.70	Normality Well Within Limits

Table A.2

First Iteration of Delphi Technique with Respect to "Dimensions of Gold Futures" of the volatility in the bullion market (No. of Experts = 10)

Summary of First Iteration				
Sl. No.	**Category**	**Details**	**Mean % Agreement**	**Remarks**
1	Factors	Dimensions, Motivational Factor	67.40	Disagreement on nature of "Motivational" Factor
2	Items	18	75.12	Disagreement on "Span of Attention" of Respondents
3	"Normality" Conformance	Based on Pilot Study of 80 Ss	54.20	Normality not within agreeable limits
Summary of Second Iteration				
Sl. No.	**Category**	**Details**	**Mean % Agreement**	**Remarks**
1	Factors	Dimensions and "Motivation" Factor merged	77.20	"Motivation" Factor Merged with Other Factors
2	Items	14	78.80	Common and Irrelevant Items Reduced
3	"Normality" Conformance	Based on Pilot Study of 80 Ss	66.70	Levels of Normality May be Improved
Summary of Third Iteration				
Sl. No.	**Category**	**Details**	**Mean % Agreement**	**Remarks**
1	Factors	Four widely observed Dimensions	90.40	Factors Further Refined to Maintain Distinction
2	Items	8	88.80	Common and Irrelevant Items Further Reduced
3	"Normality" Conformance	Based on Pilot Study of 80 Ss	89.70	Normality Well Within Limits

Factor Analysis
TABLE A.3
ANALYSIS FOR 22 VARIABLES OF INFLUENCING FACTORS SCALE OF VOLATILITY IN THE BULLION MARKET

Empirical Upper Bound for the First Eigenvalue =7.637
Chi-square Test that All Eigenvalues are Equal
$N_{Pilot\text{-}Study}$ = 80, Chi-square = 2986.297, df = 23.000, p-value = 0.0001
Chi-square Test that the Last 14 Eigenvalues are Equal
$N_{Pilot\text{-}Study}$ = 80, Chi-square – 8,972.227, df = 12.434, p-value = 0.000

Rotated Loading Matrix (VARIMAX, Gamma = 1.000000)

	1	2	3	4	5	6	7	8
ITEM 1	**0.844**	-0.069	-0.072	0.161	-0.117	0.076	-0.078	-0.068
ITEM 2	**0.812**	0.004	0.046	-0.149	0.074	0.071	0.127	0.082
ITEM 3	**0.811**	0.095	0.179	0.055	0.149	0.051	-0.080	-0.065
ITEM 4	**0.808**	0.023	0.010	0.001	-0.356	0.129	0.131	0.097
ITEM 5	**0.800**	-0.022	0.178	-0.056	0.120	-0.011	0.012	-0.023
ITEM 6	**0.797**	0.027	0.099	-0.087	-0.066	0.187	0.109	-0.033
ITEM 7	-0.122	**0.862**	0.091	-0.039	0.047	0.122	0.038	0.059
ITEM 8	0.249	**0.846**	0.090	0.047	-0.117	0.218	-0.050	0.229
ITEM 9	-0.127	**0.819**	0.084	0.122	-0.094	0.079	0.092	0.035
ITEM 10	0.256	**0.812**	0.082	0.213	0.175	0.072	0.255	-0.122
ITEM 11	0.038	0.055	**0.894**	0.024	0.038	-0.140	-0.068	0.114
ITEM 12	-0.108	-0.047	**0.824**	0.107	-0.075	0.151	0.197	0.156
ITEM 13	0.073	0.001	0.075	**0.860**	0.053	0.108	0.153	0.406
ITEM 14	-0.113	-0.149	-0.032	**0.817**	0.076	0.115	0.163	0.106
ITEM 15	-0.121	0.362	0.006	-0.070	**0.933**	0.059	0.270	0.186
ITEM 16	0.084	0.202	0.081	-0.055	**0.833**	0.056	0.001	-0.094
ITEM 17	0.117	-0.088	0.285	0.078	-0.037	**0.875**	-0.141	0.073
ITEM 18	-0.024	0.103	0.124	0.015	0.132	**0.825**	0.035	0.089
ITEM 19	0.014	-0.055	0.048	0.241	-0.009	0.085	**0.902**	0.009
ITEM 20	0.040	00289	0.071	0.172	0.395	0.157	**0.891**	0.125
ITEM 21	-0.045	-0.075	0.082	0.182	-0.020	-0.040	0.110	**0.898**
ITEM 22	0.093	-0.026	-0.098	-0.104	0.065	0.198	-0.035	**0.837**

"Variance" Explained by Rotated Components

1	2	3	4	5	6	7	8
2.279	3.451	3.469	1.848	1.945	2.265	1.509	1.848

Percent of Total Variance Explained

1	2	3	4	5	6	7	8	
10.361	15.688	15.769	8.400	8.841	10.297	6.858	8.400	**84.614%**

TABLE A.4

SUMMARY OF NORMALITY TESTS OF RESPONSES TO FACTORS INFLUENCING OF VOLATILITY IN THE BULLION MARKET QUESTIONNAIRE FOR THE PILOT-TEST SAMPLE ($N_{Pilot\text{-}Study} = 80$)

Sl. No.	Influencing Factors of Bullion Markets	SHAPIRO-WILK TEST (SW TEST) &&		KOLMOGOROV-SMIRNOV TEST (KS TEST) &&	
		SW Statistic	SW P-Value	KS Statistic	KS P-Value
1	Global Crisis	1.667	0.704*	0.188	0.772**
2	Inflation Rate	1.678	0.789*	0.171	0.787**
3	Value of the U.S. Dollar	1.684	0.758*	0.197	0.747**
4	Interest Rates	1.685	0.736*	0.191	0.790**
5	Consumption of Gold	1.662	0.778*	0.190	0.848**
6	Recession in world market	1.704	0.749*	0.186	0.757**
7	Gold demand and supply	1.750	0.842*	0.180	0.791**
8	REPO Rate	1.651	0.882*	0.193	0.814**

*** Not Significant at 0.05 level of Significance** **** Not Significant at 0.05 level of Significance**

&& The null hypothesis (Ho) involved is "there is NO deviation from expected normal distribution i.e., Dexp = 0". Non Significance indicates NOT REJECTING (Accepting) this null hypothesis.

TABLE A.5
ANALYSIS OF FACTORS INFLUENCING OF VOLATILITY IN THE BULLION MARKET QUESTIONNAIRE
($N_{Pilot\text{-}Study} = 80$)

Sl. No.	Influencing Factors of Bullion Markets	Mean	Standard Deviation	Number of Items	Mean Inter Item Correlation	Cronbach's Alpha
1	Global Crisis	18.321	2.805	6	0.785	0.956
2	Inflation Rate	13.100	1.881	4	0.742	0.920
3	Value of the U.S. Dollar	5.601	1.196	2	0.790	0.883
4	Interest Rates	6.076	1.307	2	0.730	0.844
5	Consumption of Gold	5.772	1.479	2	0.792	0.884
6	Recession in world market	5.319	1.624	2	0.821	0.902
7	Gold demand and supply	6.345	1.665	2	0.812	0.896
8	REPO Rate	5.726	1.095	2	0.882	0.937
SCALE DETAILS						
9	**Alpha Odd Items**	0.874	-	-	-	-
10	**Alpha Even Items**	0.844	-	-	-	-
11	**Alpha All Items**	0.812	-	-	-	-
12	**Spearman-Brown**	0.867	-	-	-	-
13	**Guttman Coeff.**	0.879	-	-	-	-
14	**Split-Half Coeff.**	0.923	-	-	-	-
15	***Mean Concurrent Validity***		0.887			

TABLE A.6
FACTOR ANALYSIS FOR 8 VARIABLES OF DIMENSIONS SCALE OF VOLATILITY IN THE BULLION MARKET

Empirical Upper Bound for the First Eigenvalue = 2.762

Chi-square Test that All Eigenvalues are Equal
$N_{Pilot\text{-}Study}$ = 80, Chi-square = 391.908, df = 20.000, p-value = 0.0001

Chi-square Test that the Last 4 Eigenvalues are Equal
$N_{Pilot\text{-}Study}$ = 80, Chi-square – 50.352, df = 6.055, p-value = 0.000

Rotated Loading Matrix (VARIMAX, Gamma = 1.000000)

	1	2	3	4
ITEM 1	**0.795**	0.162	0.009	0.085
ITEM 2	**0.754**	-0.051	0.038	0.225
ITEM 3	-0.098	**0.852**	-0.060	0.153
ITEM 4	0.033	**0.780**	0.166	-0.036
ITEM 5	0.278	-0.063	**0.785**	0.105
ITEM 6	-0.075	0.119	**0.752**	0.153
ITEM 7	0.134	-0.068	0.091	**0.852**
ITEM 8	0.177	0.105	0.167	**0.706**

"Variance" Explained by Rotated Components

1	2	3	4
1.524	1.366	1.155	1.342

Percent of Total Variance Explained

1	2	3	4	
19.050	17.075	14.431	16.778	67.334%

TABLE A.7

SUMMARY OF NORMALITY TESTS OF RESPONSES TO DIMENSIONS OF GOLD FUTURES OF VOLATILITY IN THE BULLION MARKET QUESTIONNAIRE FOR THE PILOT-TEST SAMPLE ($N_{Pilot\text{-}Study} = 80$)

Sl. No.	Dimension of Gold Futures Questionnaire	SHAPIRO-WILK TEST (SW TEST) &&		KOLMOGOROV-SMIRNOV TEST (KS TEST) &&	
		SW Statistic	SW P-Value	KS Statistic	KS P-Value
1	Functional Dimension	1.221	0.872*	0.236	0.702**
2	Demographic Dimension	1.378	0.817*	0.207	0.717**
3	Opportunity Dimension	1.484	0.768*	0.257	0.757**
4	Financial Dimension	1.485	0.833*	0.229	0.719**

*** Not Significant at 0.05 level of Significance** **** Not Significant at 0.05 level of Significance**

&& The null hypothesis (Ho) involved is "there is NO deviation from expected normal distribution i.e., Dexp = 0". Non Significance indicates NOT REJECTING (Accepting) this null hypothesis.

TABLE A.8
ANALYSIS OF DIMENSIONS OF GOLD FUTURES OF VOLATILITY IN THE BULLION MARKET QUESTIONNAIRE ($N_{Pilot\text{-}Study} = 80$)

Sl. No.	Dimension of Gold Futures Questionnaire	Mean	Standard Deviation	Number of Items	Mean Inter Item Correlation	Cronbach's Alpha
1	Functional Dimension	5.435	1.227	2	0.785	0.881
2	Demographic Dimension	5.576	1.391	2	0.742	0.852
3	Opportunity Dimension	5.781	1.258	2	0.790	0.883
4	Financial Dimension	6.099	1.412	2	0.730	0.844
SCALE DETAILS						
5	**Alpha Odd Items**	0.843	-	-	-	-
6	**Alpha Even Items**	0.852	-	-	-	-
7	**Alpha All Items**	0.872	-	-	-	-
8	**Spearman-Brown**	0.868	-	-	-	-
9	**Guttman Coeff.**	0.847	-	-	-	-
10	**Split-Half Coeff.**	0.893	-	-	-	-
11	*Mean Concurrent Validity*		0.893			

Hence to conclude, this chapter covers the summary of data analysis by employing various statistical techniques and methods to obtain the hidden patterns with respect to dimensions of gold futures with special reference to bullion market for establishing hypothesis and achieving the objective of research study.

CHAPTER - 6

SUMMARY OF FINDINGS, CONCLUSION AND SUGGESTIONS

In this chapter, the summary of findings, conclusion and suggestions are listed by considering the title of the research study and all objectives of the study.

6.1 Summary of Findings

The findings of the study are listed with respect to each individual objective of the study. The findings of the study are summarized in the following points:

Findings based on the objective no. 1: To study and understand the volatility in the bullion market with respect to gold.

(i) The research work was an opportunity to study and understand the volatility in the bullion market with respect to gold. Various drivers of gold futures were identified like Government policy, Market conditions, Globalization, Price volatility, Economic condition and Technological advancement.

(ii) The commonly observed influencing factors of volatility in the bullion market are "Global Crisis", "Inflation Rate", "Value of the U.S. Dollar", "Interest Rates", "Consumption of Gold", "Recession in world market" "Gold demand and supply" and "REPO Rate".

Findings based on the Objective 2: To identify various risks factors that are to be addressed in view of the volatility.

(i) The perception of risk factors by investors were identified as hedging tool, Assured Returns, Liquidity, Speculation, Arbitrage and Individual risk. Similarly, various risks factors were identified by talking to Export market expert, Investors of Gold Futures, Gold Dealers and Stock Brokers.

(ii) The commonly observed risks factors that are to be addressed in view of the volatility are "Functional Risk", "Demographic Risk", "Prospect Risk" and "Financial Risk".

(iii) The experts' opinion summarizes the Industrial Usage and Individual Usage of gold that represent the "Functional Risk" of gold futures.

(iv) The Frequency of Occurrence in Percentage of Functional Risk was 42 percent with special reference to gold futures.

(v) The experts' opinion summarizes the Degree of Savings and Long term investment plan related to gold that represent the "Demographic Risk" of gold futures.

(vi) The Frequency of Occurrence in Percentage of Demographic Risk was 27 percent with special reference to gold futures.

Findings based on the Objective 3: To examine the hedging mechanism to counter various risks associated with volatility.

(i) Various hedging mechanism were extracted by talking to Export market expert, Investors of Gold Futures, Gold Dealers and Stock Brokers.

(ii) The common hedging mechanism to counter various risks associated with volatility are "Stocks", "Foreign exchange hedge", "Insurance", "Forward contracts", "Swaps", and "Futures contracts".

(iii) The common hedging mechanism to counter various risks associated with volatility are observed Stocks with the maximum frequency of percentage of 28, Foreign exchange hedge with 24 percentage, Insurance with 17 percentage, Forward contracts with a4 percentage, Swaps with 10 percentage and Futures contracts with 7 percentage.

Findings based on the Objective 4: To compare and contrast the dimensions of commodity futures of bullion market of select Western markets with India.

(i) The volatility linkage analyses confirm the existence of volatility transmission among the majority of the sample countries' gold futures.

(ii) The data so collected from various sources related to compare and contrast the Risks of commodity futures of bullion market of select Western markets with India.

(iii) The three main areas of commodities are food, energy, and metals. The most popular food futures are for meat, wheat, and sugar. Most energy futures are for oil and gasoline.

(iv) Metals using futures include gold, silver, and copper. The results are the risks of commodity futures of bullion market of Western markets such as USA, Germany, France and Switzerland with India.

(v) India is the country with maximum population i.e., 132.42 crores but minimum Gold Reserve of 560.3 tonnes and only 5.5% of foreign reserves.

(vi) In case of USA, the population 32.34 crores with maximum Gold Reserve of 8,133.5 tonnes and 75.2% of foreign reserves.

(vii) In case of Germany, the population 8.27 crores with Gold Reserve of 3,371.0 tonnes and 70.6% of foreign reserves.

(viii) In case of France, the population 6.69 crores with the Gold Reserve of 2,436.0 tonnes and 63.9% of foreign reserves.

(ix) In case of Switzerland, the population 8.42 crores with the Gold Reserve of 1040.00 tonnes and 54.2% of foreign reserves.

Based on the above result, the commodity futures of bullion market of Western markets are highly risk comparable to Indian market. India is market for the commodity futures of bullion market with good opportunities for the Investors in Gold Futures as well as for the Gold Dealers.

6.2 Conclusion

The research study was Empirical in nature and the required data were collected through experimentation or observation of the researcher. Here the responses with respect to Dimensions of Gold Futures with special reference to Bullion Market were gathered by employing stratified random sampling. The exploratory and descriptive research design was adopted due to the nature of the study.

Investing in the bullion market doesn't derive without risk due to volatility in the bullion market. A market crash could crush this investment's performance, even if the quality of the investment remains the same since investments also follow trends. But the Indian Investors especially Investment in Gold is crazier to take risk and ready invest in Gold Futures. The problem that insistently faces the Indian investment companies is the price uncertainty of scraps in the market owing to fiscal, economic and political factors. The price movements in bullion markets in India are neither precisely cyclical nor precisely lateral and have been known to defy any binary relationship of cause and effect. Thus Gold future contracts are very important tool for risk management. Hence they are primarily used for the purpose of managing risk by those managing funds.

Trading of this instrument also allows the market participants, the opportunities of making profits either by taking risk i.e., speculation or simultaneously taking opposite position in the spot and future markets, or in the future market alone, to take advantage of price differentials i.e., arbitrage. Future contracts therefore performs the functions of price discovery, risk transfer and market completion.

6.3 Suggestions

In this chapter, the researcher has given important suggestions to the related sectors which can be implemented in the broader area to the bullion markets. The important suggestions are listed below:

6.3.1 The drivers of gold futures such as Government policy, Market conditions, Globalization, Price volatility, Economic condition and Technological advancement need to be considered while planning for investment in bullion market. The drivers vary from government policy to technological advancement.

6.3.2 The majority of the respondents were strongly agreed regarding the government policy that influence bullion market because in India the Central Government changes the business policy to strengthen the Indian Economy. Sometime, the business policy indicates in favour or against the bullion market and the business opportunities. On the other hand, around 30 percent of the respondents were strongly disagreed and were not ready to believe related to government policy and the influence on bullion market because of inadequate market information and awareness about the trends of bullion markets.

6.3.3 The investors of gold futures should consider the present government policy, market conditions and stability of the same government for the future time while deciding for investing in bullion market for short term, medium or long term. Similarly, the gold dealers should consider the drivers of gold futures such as Government policy, Market conditions, Globalization, Price volatility, Economic condition and Technological advancement while planning for investment in bullion market.

6.3.4 Investment in the bullion market doesn't derive without risk due to volatility in the bullion market. So, the perceptions of risk factors by investors which were identified through the outcome of semi-structured interview schedule. The perceptions of risk factors by investors are Hedging Tool, Assured Returns, Liquidity, Speculation, Arbitrage and Individual risk. These risk factors vary from hedging tool to individual risk. The majority percentage of respondent was strongly aware about the investing and its risk factors especially in bullion market. The rest of the respondents have given their mixed opinion regarding the investing and its risk factors especially in bullion market.

6.3.5 When the investors in gold futures and gold dealers are aware about the risk factors, should take the required precautions for handling those risks. The gold dealers should share the real time market conditions with the investors of gold futures to safeguard their investment. The Dealers can make efforts to educate existing as well as prospective customers about their offerings thus create customer awareness about other services offered and improve trade for those services.

6.3.6 The factors that influence the volatility in the bullion market with respect to Gold were extracted by talking to Stock market expert, Investors of Gold Futures, Gold Dealers and Stock Brokers. The opinion of majority of the respondents indicates that the Global Crisis is the factor influences the volatility in the bullion market with respect to gold. So, the investors of gold futures and gold dealers should update regularly the real-time information related to world market condition especially bullion market. According to the respondents the changes of Inflation Rate is another factor that influences the volatility in the bullion market with respect to gold. The experts have given their first preferences around 18 percent of respondents.

6.3.7 When inflation rate increases the gold price decreases. In another way as the money supply increases, the price of the gold raises. Value of the U.S. Dollar is the factor that influences the volatility in the bullion market with respect to gold. If gold price raise against the US Dollar, gold becomes more expensive for the buyers around the world as gold is Dollar denominated. REPO Rate is the factor that influences the volatility in the bullion market with respect to gold. When the REPO rate increases, the borrowing from the banks decreases which actually reduces the purchasing power of the public and leads to reduce the investment in Gold and will reduces the price of Gold.

6.3.8 The commonly observed risks factors that are to be addressed in view of the volatility are "Functional Risk", "Demographic Risk", "Prospect Risk" and "Financial Risk". The experts' opinion summarizes the Industrial Usage and Individual Usage of gold that represent the Functional Risk of gold futures. Gold alloys are used for fillings, crowns, bridges and orthodontic appliances. Gold is used in density because it is chemically inert, non-allergenic and easy for the dentist to work. When the industrial usage of gold increases, the price also increases that indicates the investment of gold becomes more secure and beneficial. The experts' opinion summarizes the Degree of

Savings and Long term investment plan related to gold that represent the Demographic Risk of gold futures. Based on the gold price trends and market value of gold in future, investment in gold for long term is secured and profitable.

6.3.9 The hedging mechanism to counter various risks associated with volatility. Various hedging mechanism to counter various risks associated with volatility are "Stocks", "Foreign exchange hedge", "Insurance", "Forward contracts", "Swaps", and "Futures contracts". Investment especially for long term is unpredictable and uncertain. But several hedging mechanisms that can be helpful to counter various risks associated with volatility. Employ dedicated advisors for the customers where in a group of customers are handled by the advisor and similarly there can be a few advisors handling a few customers.

6.3.10 The degree of difficulties levels encountered in changing the existing behaviour of Investors of Gold Futures, Gold Dealers and Stock Brokers. The results point out the comparison of basic statistics among different category of respondents with respect to different causal factors. The CV values of various factors i.e., Global Crisis, Inflation Rate, Interest Rate and REPO Rates are less than 0.25 in the *Investors of Gold Futures* point of view. There is no significant level of difficulties in changing the factors that influence the volatility in the bullion market with respect to gold.

The CV values of all factors i.e., Global Crisis, Inflation Rate, Value of the U.S. Dollar, Interest Rate, Consumption of Gold, Recession in world market, Gold demand and supply and REPO Rates are less than 0.25 in the *Gold Dealers* point of view. The results indicate there is no significant level of difficulties in changing the factors that influence the volatility in the bullion market with respect to gold.

The CV values of all influencing factors Global Crisis, Inflation Rate, Value of the U.S. Dollar, Interest Rate, Consumption of Gold, Recession in world market, Gold demand and supply and REPO Rates are less than 0.25 in the *Stock Brokers* point of view. The results indicate there is no significant level of difficulties in changing the factors that influence the volatility in the bullion market with respect to gold.

6.3.11 The degree of difficulties levels indicates the comparison of basic statistics among different category of respondents with respect to the Risks of Gold Futures. The CV values of Risks of Gold Futures i.e., Functional Risk, Demographic Risk, Prospect Risk and Financial Risk are more than 0.25 in the Investors of Gold Futures point of view. The results indicate there is significant level of difficulties in adjusting with the Risks of Gold Futures with special reference to bullion market.

The CV values of Risks of Gold Futures i.e., Functional Risk, Demographic Risk, Prospect Risk and Financial Risk are less than 0.25 in the Gold Dealers point of view. The results consider there is no significant level of difficulties in adjusting with the Risks of Gold Futures with special reference to bullion market.

The CV values of Risks of Gold Futures i.e., Functional Risk, Demographic Risk, Prospect Risk and Financial Risk are less than 0.25 in the Stock Brokers point of view. The results consider there is no significant level of difficulties in adjusting with the Risks of Gold Futures with special reference to bullion market.

6.3.12 The summary of level of difficulties in changing the hedging mechanism to counter various risks associated with volatility from the view point of concerned stakeholders. The hedging mechanism to counter various risks associated with volatility categories into two such as Quantity Related mechanism and Quality Related mechanism. The CV values of Risks associated with volatility i.e., Quantity Related mechanism and Quality Related mechanism are less than 0.25 in the Investors in *Gold Futures, Gold Dealers and Stock Brokers* point of view. The results consider there is no significant level of difficulties in changing the hedging mechanism to counter various risks associated with volatility.

6.3.13 Risk tolerance is the degree of variability in investment returns that an investor is willing to withstand. This should have a realistic understanding of the ability and willingness to stomach large swings in the value of the investments; if you take on too much risk, you might panic and sell at the wrong time. It was revealed in the table that out of 650 respondents, 380 forming 58.46 % possessed a very high level of Risk Tolerance and 186 respondents forming 28.61% possessed average risk tolerance. The remaining 84 respondents neither possessed moderately low tolerance (30 respondents) and very low risk tolerance (54 respondents).

6.3.14 The results are the risks of commodity futures of bullion market of Western markets such as USA, Germany, France and Switzerland with India. India is the country with maximum population i.e., 132.42 crores but minimum Gold Reserve of 560.3 tonnes and only 5.5% of foreign reserves. In case of USA, the population 32.34 crores with maximum Gold Reserve of 8,133.5 tonnes and 75.2% of foreign reserves. In case of Germany, the population 8.27 crores with Gold Reserve of 3,371.0 tonnes and 70.6% of foreign reserves. And in case of France, the population 6.69 crores with the Gold Reserve of 2,436.0 tonnes and 63.9% of foreign reserves.

Based on the above result, the commodity futures of bullion market of Western markets are highly risk comparable to Indian market. India is the market for the commodity futures of bullion with good opportunities for the Investors in Gold Futures as well as for the Gold Dealers. So, the investors in gold futures and gold dealers are in the main stream in Indian Bullion Markets. The company can simplify the online user interface with the aid of external technical expert and provide regular updates about the markets, their account and also guide them with their trade.

6.3.15 The Gold Dealers can turn non-active customers into active customers interacting with them on a regular basis and further guiding them by solving their problems or issues. The Gold Dealers can introduce monthly trading guides that would exclusively talk about the hedging, arbitrage and speculation strategies. This will promote investors knowledge in the equity trading and also ensure customer loyalty; further enhancing the company's reputation as an investment advisors.

6.4 SCOPE OF THE FURTHER RESEARCH

Investing in the bullion market doesn't derive without risk due to volatility in the bullion market. A market crash could crush this investment's performance, even if the quality of the investment remains the same since investments also follow trends. The present study was to identify the issues related to the volatility in the bullion market with respect to gold and find out various risks factors that are to be addressed in view of the volatility. There are several issues could not address in the research study that creates the scope of further research are as follows:

1. Limited Scope of Research Area: The present research study was limited to Karnataka state only but the research can be done throughout India with larger sample size for getting better and more realistic outcome.

2. Investing in physical gold: The research study was considered the physical gold only but can be considered on virtual gold investment and Gold Exchange Traded Fund. The further research can be concentrated on the relevant questions like, Should you invest in physical gold? What are the risks with respect to physical gold in future?

3. Equity based Gold Funds: There is a scope of further research on Equity based Gold Funds. Here these funds are directly not investing in Gold but investing in the companies, which are related to the mining, extracting and marketing of the Gold. Besides, its performance is purely dependent upon the performance of the fund house and the equities they are investing.

4. Research on E-Gold: In India, E-gold is a good option for the investors without having physical gold and caring the risk of storing. E-gold is held electronically in the demat form and can be freely converted into physical gold. In India, e-gold is offered by the National Spot Exchange Limited (NSEL), which gives investors the option to invest in commodities such as gold, silver and platinum online.

CPSIA information can be obtained
at www.ICGtesting.com
Printed in the USA
LVHW112038270323
742731LV00020BA/556

9 787113 250744